"In wonderfully understandable and concise language, Bob Guess has presented what every senior citizen needs to know to keep from jeopardizing their retirement or estate. The topics are so well laid out that I venture to say it's a fun read."

-David Ramsour, PhD

International Economist and Financial Consultant

"I love the clear, fiery writing, the detail, the good news, the suggestions for... what to do to make things better!"

- Brett Williams, PhD

Author of *Debt For Sale*

ROBBED
with a Pen Again

A GUIDE TO PROTECTING YOUR ASSETS

A GUIDE TO PROTECTING YOUR ASSETS

ROBBED
with a Pen Again

BOB GUESS

Restoring America

Robbed With a Pen Again: A Guide to Protecting Your Assets by Bob Guess
Copyright © 2008 Bob Guess
Copyright © 2014 Bob Guess
Copyright © 2016 Bob Guess

2016 Edition

All rights reserved. No part of this book may be used or reproduced in any manner whatsoever without written permission from the author except in the case of brief quotations embodied in critical articles and reviews.

Company and product names mentioned herein are the trademarks or registered trademarks of their respective owners.

For information regarding special discounts for bulk purchases, please contact Texas First Financial at 866-590-2555 or visit texas1stfinancial.com.

Published by
Restoring America
P.O. Box 1328
Van Alstyne, Texas 75495

Library of Congress Control Number: 2016936628
ISBN: 978-0-9974260-0-7
Business & Economics / Personal Finance / Money Management / Retirement Planning

The information in this book does not render legal advice
or operate as a substitute for legal counsel.

Printed in the United States of America

Contents

AUTHOR'S NOTE . . . . *ix*

1   WHY ROBBED WITH A PEN AGAIN? 1
    *"In times of unusual deceit, telling the truth will be a
    revolutionary act."* –George Orwell

2   BANKS: THE EVIL EMPIRE? 9
    *"The great enemy of the truth is very often not the lie—deliberate,
    contrived, and dishonest—but the myth—persistent, persuasive and
    unrealistic."* –John F. Kennedy

3   CREDIT CARD COMPANIES: LEGALIZED MAFIA? 27
    *"If you have integrity nothing else matters, if you don't have
    integrity nothing else matters."*
    –Alan K. Simpson, U. S. Senator, Wyoming

4   ANNUITIES: THE GOOD, THE BAD AND THE UGLY . . . 45
    "Some will rob you with a six-gun, and some with a fountain pen."
    –Woody Guthrie

5   LIFE SETTLEMENTS VS. VIATICALS 73
    Why would I want to purchase a life insurance policy as
    part of my investment portfolio?

6   HOW TO PROTECT YOURSELF FROM IDENTITY THEFT
    WITHOUT IT COSTING YOU AN ARM AND A LEG. 77

7 REVERSE MORTGAGES: BUYERS BEWARE. 81
"Truth fears no questions." –Unknown

8 LONG-TERM CARE: IS IT RIGHT FOR ME? 97
"Life is filled with golden opportunities carefully disguised as irresolvable problems." –John Gardner, former Secretary of State

9 THE MEDICAID SPEND-DOWN PROCESS: PROTECTING WHAT YOU'VE SPENT A LIFETIME ACCUMULATING . .107
"Talk is cheap... except when Congress does it." –Mark Twain

10 STRETCH IRAS: HOW TO CREATE WEALTH AND PASS IT TO YOUR HEIRS 121
"Man's mind, stretched to a new idea, never goes back to its original dimension." –Oliver Wendell Holmes

11 WILLS VS. RECOVABLE LIVING TRUSTS: HOW TO PREVENT HEIR-TO-HEIR COMBAT! 129
"It's not that I'm afraid to die; I just don't want to be there when it happens." –Woody Allen

12 INVESTMENT ADVISOR OR BROKER: WHO SHOULD I CHOOSE TO INVEST MY MONEY? 141
"Forecasting can be difficult; especially if it concerns the future."
–Robert Kiyosaki

13 ARMED AND DANGEROUS: THE "TEN SAFEGUARDS"..151
"They must find it difficult...Those who have taken authority as the truth, rather than truth as the authority." –Gerald Massey

GLOSSARY 161
RESOURCES 171
ACKNOWLEDGMENTS cxci

Author's Note

There are always new and *creative* ways agents, advisors, and bankers attempt to scam you for your money. As Woodie Guthrie sings, "Some will rob you with a six-gun, and some with a fountain pen."

When I began working in this industry very little information from outside sources was available. Information about annuity products was primarily industry literature. I was "indoctrinated" by the best trainers the insurance industry had to offer. I have learned the mistakes pointed out in this book from firsthand experience.

After being in the industry for a few years, an opportunity to teach continuing education courses at multiple college campuses motivated me to do more research about insurance products and financial investment business practices. In the process, along with input from students, I had to face a difficult truth: I could not reconcile my business experience with the truth that my research revealed. Standing before a class of senior adults—many of whom had been victimized because of their lack of knowledge—caused me to make a paradigm shift in my thought processes, philosophy, and practices. I had no choice. I had to swim against the current. It was the right thing to do. I gained these insights in order to educate and empower the consumer.

You spent a lifetime accumulating your assets so you can retire with a sense of dignity; this is vital to your peace of mind. Senior adults control 70% of our nation's wealth, but are also the most-targeted by the financially dishonest.

I will show you how you can keep yourself from being scammed by financial predators and reveal some of the latest ways the industry and agents attempt to deceive you with high-commission products. I'll identify these financial predators through a breakdown of the 2008 financial crisis. Get ready for the ride of your life as we pull back the curtain on financial predators and explore the true investment opportunities that will allow you to protect and preserve what you have spent a lifetime accumulating.

Bob Guess
Van Alstyne, Texas

CHAPTER ONE

Why *Robbed with a Pen* Again?

"In times of unusual deceit, telling the truth will be a revolutionary act."

–George Orwell

DO YOU REMEMBER LIFE before the first personal computer rolled off an IBM assembly line? Do you remember the eradication of smallpox and the identification of AIDS? Do you remember former President Ronald Reagan simultaneously denouncing "the Evil Empire" and announcing the "Star Wars missile defense system"? Do you remember the 2008 financial crisis? Do you remember, from the luxurious perch of hindsight, your personal tale of some charlatan who attempted to rob you with a pen?

I recently met with a woman who was panic-stricken because she could not access her money. A salesman masquerading as an investment advisor tied up every penny she had in annuities without her realizing the consequences of this decision. She will incur heavy penalties if she tries to access over 10% of her money. At the time she purchased the investment, she had no idea this decision would leave her with no operating capital or savings. *This is being robbed with a pen.*

On top of that, another salesman–preying on her desperation–attempted to sell her a reverse mortgage to "free up" the cash for living expenses. He hounded her for weeks. Fortunately, before making her final decision, she tuned in to our radio program, *Dollars & Sense*. On this particular day we were discussing the good, the bad, and the ugly of reverse mortgages. After listening to the program, she realized once again that she was being misled.

INTEGRITY FRAUD

There has never been another time in American history when there were so many incompetent people after your money. Most salespeople competing for your investment dollars are not trained as legitimate Investment Advisors. *They are not qualified to help you make profitable financial decisions.*

> **There has never been a time in American history when there were so many incompetent people going after your money.**

When you look up the word "integrity" you will find it means "wholeness derived from honesty and consistent uprightness of character." You will also find the basic definition for fraud is "a deception made for personal gain." Playwright and author William Saroyan once said, "Good people are good because they've come to wisdom through failure." People who have not "come to wisdom" are the ones who commit integrity fraud. They do *not* have wholeness derived from consistent and upright behavior. Their blatant disregard for others causes them to continue to deceive people for personal gain while justifying their every action.

> *Good people are good because they've come to wisdom through failure.*
> -William Saroyan, playwright

RESPONSIBLE INTEGRITY

Nurturing and protecting the nest egg you have worked so hard to accumulate will demand that you step up to the plate and make wise, intelligent decisions.

I've worked in the financial services arena for more than 35 years, and have watched the aging of America and the subsequent increase in their retirement assets over those years. Since the inception of tax-deferred retirement accounts in 1974, I have seen many IRA balances grow from the tens of thousands to over three million dollars. In today's economic environment, if you follow the advice of disinformation specialists you could easily run through your entire life's savings.

Let's cut through all the hocus-pocus and fear tactics that many so-called experts use to manipulate you. This book can empower you to truly control your own financial destiny!

Do you remember the old TV program, *To Tell the Truth*? The basic premise of the program revolved around three contestants claiming to be the same person. A panel asked questions in an attempt to identify truth in the midst of impostors. At the end of the program the moderator said, "Will the real _____ please stand up?" The real person stood (usually after some playful false starts), and once we knew who the real person was, the two impostors revealed their true identities.

Wouldn't it be nice if it were that easy to tell who is actually qualified to handle your money and identify the real impostors? "Will the real Registered Investment Advisor please stand up?"

> *It's time for greatness, not greed.*
> -Marian Wright Edelman

This is a straightforward, "tell-it-like-it-is" guide to help you navigate through a maze designed to confuse you. By the time you finish reading you will be able to differentiate between a trustworthy Investment Advisor and a glorified salesman who wants to get rich at your expense.

Almost every educational manual written for salespeople in the financial services industry teaches them how to separate you from your money. Entire books are devoted to understanding the psychology of senior adults and how to out leverage the competition to make a sale. You, the consumer, are nothing more than a pawn manipulated on their chessboard.

This book provides you with the knowledge (*what* to do), the confidence (*when* to do it) and the wisdom (with *whom* to do it) to control your own financial destiny.

THE POWER OF DISINFORMATION

There is an ongoing WAR for your money and the strategy being used is the same in almost every case. It is an ancient strategy that can be boiled down to one word: DISINFORMATION.

Disinformation: the *deliberate* use of misleading information in order to deceive the public.

Disinformation is a strategy of war and politics. Politicians call it "spin." Disinformation is an effective weapon against belief systems. It is most dangerous when it contains a seed of truth. The use of disinformation to manipulate public opinion is a highly developed art. It is well understood by the national security establishment as well as among marketing and public relations wizards who choose to use *deception* instead of truth.

Senior adults control 70% of our nation's wealth, and therefore, are a target for disinformation specialists. These specialists can be found in the marketing departments and boardrooms of most insurance companies, credit card companies, and local and national banks. They create products loaded with disinformation geared to line the pockets of their board of directors. These products typically generate exorbitant commissions for their agents at your expense.

My purpose is not just to expose the disinformation strategies of insurance companies, banks, brokerage firms, reverse mortgage companies, credit card companies and much more, but to provide you with correct information and solutions to help you protect and preserve what you've spent a lifetime accumulating.

DON'T BE SO TRUSTING!

Over the last several years, I have taught financial stewardship classes entitled "Senior Survival," later changed to "Dollars and Sense," in the Continuing Education Program on several college campuses. My classroom experience as an instructor has proven to me that my students (mostly retirees) are *alarmingly* trusting. Many of them believed the first person who came along with fancy letterhead and counterfeit credentials behind their name printed on a business card. A substantial number of my students were tricked into buying a product (usually some form of an annuity) that did not suit their investment goals or needs.

What I have also discovered is that most senior adults have trusted their investments to inexperienced brokers. When the market turned south, they were told to "hold on until it all turns around," which assumes their investments were worth holding on to in the first place. Most of the seniors saw dramatic losses in their portfolios, panicked, and sold at a considerable loss. Making things worse, seniors began responding to the "snake oil" ads in the local newspapers, telemarketing solicitations, or direct marketing postcards inviting them to come for a "free" dinner. Statements such as, "Get All The Gains of the Stock Market Without Any Risk To Your Principle" or "First Year Bonus of 10% or More," brought seniors out by the thousands.

Does this sound familiar?

The insurance industry recognized the vacuum created by the events of the 2008 stock market correction, which many called the Great Recession. The industry immediately moved to fill the void and offered to "come to your rescue," but in reality they were like big sharks looking for fresh meat. They knew how to persuade you to take the bait, and realized you wouldn't be aware of the consequences until it was too late.

> **This book is in opposition to most of the financial industry's pundits.**

My goal is to equip you with the insight necessary to identify insurance agents selling *only* annuities, retail brokers and banks selling front-end loaded mutual funds, variable annuity salesmen promising "too good to be true" investment returns and much more.

This book is in opposition to most of the financial industry's pundits. Their "insights" are generally designed to spoon-feed you their agenda-driven pabulum. *The result is you being robbed with a pen.*

Throughout this book, you will learn from the collective expertise of such people as Arthur Levitt, former Chairman of the United States Securities and Exchange Commission; John C. Bogle, founder and retired CEO of the Vanguard Financial Group; and Warren Buffet, founder of Berkshire Hathaway Inc. These are men of substantial renown and integrity. They possess keen insight into the financial services industry.

Take a deep breath and relax. You need *never* fall victim to the "power sell" again. *Robbed with a Pen Again* is the ammunition you've been looking for to protect your nest egg!

CHAPTER TWO

BANKS: THE EVIL EMPIRE?

The great enemy of the truth is very often not the lie—deliberate, contrived, and dishonest—but the myth—persistent, persuasive and unrealistic.

—John F. Kennedy

REMEMBER THE GOOD OLE days when the president of your local bank was totally accessible? It was a time when your banker actually knew you. He knew what you did for a living. He even knew your spouse's name by heart. You saw your banker as someone you could trust, someone who could help in time of need. Your banker and his assistants were courteous and knowledgeable. Upon opening an account, you could receive a gift of CorningWare® or maybe even a free toaster. There were no monthly fees, no "gotchas" and few hidden agendas. Usually it was a pleasant experience with trustworthy people.

America used to be the land of the free. Now it's the land of the fee.

—Emily Thornton, *Business Week*

Welcome to banking in the 21st century, where the convenience of online banking and debit cards come charges and fees from every direction:

- Account set up fees.
- Monthly access fees.
- Bounced check fees.
- Insufficient funds fees. (Some banks charge as much as $45 for each overdrawn transaction.)
- ATM fees.
- Stop payment fees.
- Wire transfer fees.
- Cashier's checks and money order fees.

The cost of each fee and the creation of new fees has skyrocketed over the last few years. On May 21, 2007, *MSN Money* published an excellent article by Liz Pulliam Weston entitled, "When Banks Turn Evil." The article explores some of the insidious ways banks extract their fees. She even names some of the banks and offers solutions to fight back. According to investment banker Robert Hammer, the fees charged by banks were expected to top $55 billion in 2007 alone.

The man who has won millions at the cost of his conscience is a failure.

—B.C. Forbes

BANKING HISTORY

In 1933, Congress passed the Glass-Steagall Act, which *prohibited* commercial banks from collaborating with full-service brokerage firms or participating in investment banking activities.

America experienced an influx of legislative and regulatory changes which swept through Congress between 1980 and 1994. Highly placed executives with questionable motives sought to repeal the Act, which would have allowed them to access the personal information of account holders. These changes amended the Federal Securities and Banking Laws within the banking, brokerage, and insurance industries.

Investopedia, an investing education site, states:

"The Glass-Steagall Act was enacted during the Great Depression. It protected bank depositors from the additional risks associated with security transactions. The Act was dismantled on November 12, 1999 with the Gramm-Leach-Bliley Financial Services Modernization Act, or GLB Act. Consequently, the distinction between services offered by commercial banks and brokerage firms was *blurred.*"

In her book, *Debt for Sale: A Social History of the Credit Trap*,

Brett Williams pinpoints the power that banks hold due to the elimination of the Glass-Steagall protection:

> "One side of the firm [the bank] could consult the other about how to solve its financial difficulties, then both could agree to hide that knowledge from investors. Banks could grow even bigger and monopolize more services. Customers' personal information, including credit reports, banking history, and credit card and Social Security numbers can be shared, traded, and sold down the line. Banks can move assets into affiliates that are not required to comply with the Community Reinvestment Act. The bank side of the firm can consult insurance records in evaluating loans, disguise loans as commodity swaps, or offer insurance and make secret loans to itself."

On June 24, 1998, Ralph Nader, in testimony before the Senate Housing and Urban Affairs Committee's 3rd Hearing on H.R. 10—the Financial Services Act of 1998—delivered an insightful warning:

> "This is not a bill for consumers. It is a bill designed to create new profit centers for a relative handful of banking and financial services corporations, corporations that will form combinations which will dominate the delivery of financial products and fuel the already alarming trend toward mega mergers and the concentration of economic power."

Results of the Early Bank Mergers

David Greising, in a May 17, 1998 *Business Week* commentary, writes:

> "The abusive atmosphere at the securities division of NationsBank Corp. in the early 1990s was shocking even for veteran stockbrokers. Working at the bank's branches, they were told to hawk NationsBank investment products to bank customers without explaining that they were brokers, not bankers.... The case shows how difficult it is to regulate stockbrokers working for banks, in part because bank regulators usually lack the skills or the inclination to root out securities fraud.... Banks have pushed to stay under the umbrella of banking regulators, who have precious little experience... that's a recipe for regulatory *undersight*. It leaves regulators unable to stop sleazy selling practices by stockbrokers dressed in bankers' pinstripes."[1]

The merging of banks, brokerage firms, and insurance companies has clouded our perception of the investment world. When you walk into a bank, you need to realize that it is no longer independent, but part of a single entity with many tentacles. It has a desire to keep all your assets under one roof: its roof.

Many of the agents who work in larger banks are *captive agents*, meaning they sell you only what the bank instructs them

---

[1] David Greising, "Commentary: When Banks Act Like Brokers, Who Regulates?," *Business Week*. May 17, 1998. http://www.bloomberg.com/bw/stories/1998-05-17/commentary-when-banks-act-like-brokers-who-regulates

> When you walk into a bank, you need to realize that it is no longer independent, but part of a single entity with many tentacles. It has a desire to keep all your assets under one roof: its roof.

to sell. Most banks are set up as a *retail shop*. Their agents are not investment advisors who charge a fee, but rather represent a commission-driven banking/investment firm. Subsequently, when you purchase a mutual fund through your bank you could be charged as much as an 8.5% commission. Additionally, when you purchase an annuity at a bank *you may have a 5 to 10 year wait before you can access more than 10% of your money without a surrender penalty*!

Fee-based investment firms such as Vanguard, TD Ameritrade, Schwab Institutional, and Fidelity Investments allow you to purchase many of the same investments *without* the commissions. This allows more of your principal to be working for you. We deal with this more extensively in chapter 5.

However, firms such as Merrill Lynch, A.G. Edwards, Ameriprise Financial, and Edward Jones (your local boutique retail shop) are *not* considered registered investment advisory firms, but are similar to the banking industry. Their agents are captive agents who sell what their firms dictate and are retail shops just like banks.

Often the bank tellers are trained to steer you toward their retail investment team. It is *your* money, so be very cautious! I have included a list of valuable resources at the end of this book filled with information that will help you protect and preserve your assets.

How This New Legislation Affects Us—As Individuals and as a Nation

As a result of the Gramm-Leach-Bliley Act most banks hire securities licensed individuals or train their own staff to sell retail products to their clients. They send young trainees to securities classes to learn how to sell you annuities and mutual funds on a retail basis. This means that your investments purchased through the bank typically carry heavy commissions. (Some smaller banks hire out these services, but the agenda of the banks is clear: keep your money and make maximum profits.)

Ask yourself: "Should I trust my hard-earned dollars—all the money I have spent a *lifetime* accumulating—to someone who may be trained, but has little experience?"

Do you think the bank is going to "bail you out" if one of their new employees makes a blunder while investing your money? Money insured by the Securities Investors Protection Corporation (SIPC) does *not* protect you against poor investment advice or losses caused by a decline in the market value of your stocks, bonds, or mutual funds.

> **Along with these bank mega-mergers comes a sales force trained to keep your investment dollars with them, even though better options for you can be found elsewhere.**

Along with these bank mega-mergers comes a sales force trained to keep your investment dollars with them, even though better options for you can be found elsewhere.

The Old "Bait and Switch"

One tactic commonly used by the banking industry is the old "bait and switch." I had a client who had received an ad from her bank offering an extremely competitive rate on a 6-month CD. She, with her daughter, went to the bank to purchase the CD. After presenting the ad to the teller, they were directed over to one of the financial advisors. The financial advisor reviewed the ad and asked her, "Are tax savings important to you?" Now, who would answer "no" to this question? Pure and simple, this is the *bait* (the ad offering the 6-month CD rate) and *switch* (the tax savings question).

By answering "yes" to the banker's tax question, my client was switched to buying a 5-year annuity instead of the 6-month CD that was advertised. She wanted to talk about CDs, but the banker was only discussing annuities, which are more profitable for the bank. The annuity matched the CD rate on its first year return. However, the contract's small print revealed a reduction of the rate of return by less than half in the second through the fifth years. She did not even realize what had been done; she thought she had actually purchased a CD.

I discovered what had happened when I met with her and her daughter. I called the bank, put them on speaker phone, and requested to speak with the woman who had sold my client the 5-year annuity. They told me she was no longer employed by the bank, so I asked to speak to a supervisor. After much discussion, the bank reluctantly agreed to refund my client's money without any penalties, but basically called her a liar in the process.

WHAT ARE TRUE CONSUMER ADVOCATES SAYING ABOUT THE FINANCIAL SERVICES MODERNIZATION ACT? (COMMONLY REFERRED TO AS THE GRAMM-LEACH-BLILEY ACT)

Ed Mierzwinski is the Federal Consumer Program Director of the U.S. Public Interest Research Group (U.S. PIRG). In an October 17, 2004 interview with the PBS broadcast program, *Frontline,* Mierzwinski stated, "The Office of the Comptroller of the Currency is asleep at the switch." When it comes to protecting the consumer from banking abuse, which is the purpose of the Office of the Comptroller of the Currency, he said, "They only act when they're shamed into acting." Because the banks declined to talk to *Frontline* for the news piece, Mr. Mierzwinski was asked if the banks would talk to U.S. PIRG. "Basically," he responded, "the banks hide behind the curtain of their trade associations... to do their dirty work."

When referring to the mergers of banks, insurance companies, and stock brokerage firms and its effect on the consumer, Mr. Mierzwinski pointed out that "...your bank can share the confidential details of all of your transactions, where you use your credit card, *how much money you have in your accounts,* who are the cosigners of your accounts… any information about stocks, pensions that you have with affiliated companies. If you fill out applications with the bank, all the information that they can collect on you can be shared no matter what your choice is under federal law. California did something about that, and the Office of the Comptroller of Currency (OCC) backed the American Bankers Association in trying to defeat the law." (California opted to force banks and credit card companies to ask permission before sharing your private information.)

> *Only in America do banks leave both doors open and then chain the pens to the counters.*
>
> —Unknown

Your Bank is Not Necessarily Your Friend

Wisdom would dictate that you recognize banks may no longer be a safe place to park your money, especially after the 2008 banking crash. Banks can be predatory institutions with ulterior motives when it comes to your assets. Manage your money with that in mind. There may be people in your bank who you love to interact with, as it should be. Just remember, there are numerous layers of decision-making authority above the tellers. The deci-

> **Banks can be predatory institutions with ulterior motives regaring your assets.**

sion-makers employ powerbrokers who lobby Washington to pass laws in favor of banks. These are the very laws that often have a negative impact on your financial affairs.

Example: Banks are now mailing their customers checks. That's right—not a copy of a check, but an actual check that you can cash. What's the problem with that? Well, read their letter carefully. They want you to cash the check so that you will pay a substantial amount of interest (similar to the credit cards they peddle). They'll give you easy payments, so you will never dig your way out of the hole. Just remember: SOME BANKS ARE NOT YOUR FRIEND!

Who's Running the Federal Reserve?

Just after Federal Reserve Chairman Ben Bernanke announced the 0.5% cut in Fed interest rates, falling on the heels of the sub-prime lending debacle, Mijka Samora of the *Wall Street Journal* speculated that Mr. Bernanke may have been influenced by his discussions with bankers and other power brokers. Keep in mind that three of the five largest financial services firms in 2006 were banks: Citigroup, Bank of America, and JPMorgan Chase. This is an alarming statistic when you consider the fact that the Gramm-Leach-Bliley Act of 1999–which allowed banks and brokerage firms to merge–was less than a decade old. Samora writes:

> "The power centers of Wall Street, big banks and hedge funds, now run the Federal Reserve. There are now too many large banks and too many large hedge funds that

are too big to allow them to fail. One major failure could cascade through the system and have catastrophic consequences. How did we get there? Perhaps the repeal of Glass-Steagall and the explosive growth of unregulated hedge funds are a good explanation. None of this is a good omen for the future."[2]

THE CURRENT MARKET/BANKING CRISIS

Since the 2008 Recession the Dodd-Frank Act has regulated nearly every phase of the financial service industries, thereby driving away venture capitalists. Congress consolidated all power *within* the Federal Reserve. This is the same Federal Reserve that not only failed in its role as regulator, but contributed to the crisis by manipulating interest rates and credit qualifications. Fed chairman Alan Greenspan, in an act of severe mismanagement, lowered interest rates way below the *normal driven market range* in order to regain buoyancy in the economy. Consumer demand was low after the collapse of the tech bubble, so this was his attempt to induce spending and borrowing again. Enter the mortgage bubble.

The Federal Reserve's principal bank is headquartered in Basil, Switzerland. Their regulations on capital rules (Basil 1 & 2) gave a green light to banks, without concern for the high-risk involvement in securitized mortgages. These mortgages were financially backed by life insurance companies. The underwriting mortgage company's guidelines were lax and negligent, and

---

[2] Mijka Samora, "Who's Running the Fed," *The Wall Street Journal,* October 8, 2007.

qualified those who wouldn't normally be considered able to purchase a home. Federal Reserve banks globally led the charge toward over-leveraging in the housing markets because these mortgages were considered *safe* investments by the regulatory bodies. Everything else was a consequence. Essentially, this was just another example of a welfare program.

The Consumer Financial Protection Bureau (CFPB) that was spawned from the Dodd-Frank Act is supposed to be regulating consumer protection now. Protection from whom? Who caused this crisis, free people in the marketplace or governments and their regulatory machinery?

What is the CFPB actually doing? Monitoring all credit card transactions, and mortgage transactions by American consumers, approximately 40 *billion* transactions each year. "A CFPB strategic planning document for fiscal years 2013-17 describes the 'markets monitoring' program through which officials aim to monitor 80 percent of all credit card transactions in 2013. The U.S. Census Bureau reports that 1.16 billion consumer credit cards were in use in 2012 for an estimated 52.6 billion transactions. If CFPB officials reach their stated 'performance goal,' they would collect data on 42 billion transactions made with 933 million credit cards used by American consumers."[3]

Behavioral law is a *nirvana* approach to economic growth. It pretends to remove risk in the name of consumer protection. It grows government and creates the groundwork for corpo-

---

[3] Richard Polluck, "CFPB's data-mining on consumer credit cards challenged in heated House hearing," *Washington Examiner*, September 13, 2013. http://www.washingtonexaminer.com/cfpbs-data-mining-on-consumer-credit-cards-challenged-in-heated-house-hearing/article/2535726

rate-government corruption.

> *"...liberty and privacy are two sides of the same coin."*[4]
> -William H. Peterson, Economist

When people say that the financial sector has been deregulated, I just laugh and shake my head. The financial sector is more entangled with government than *any* other sector of our economy. Surveillance has moved beyond anything we could have imagined with the NSA. No one's personal habits are confidential with the Consumer Financial Protection Bureau. Freedom of information is scoffed at by government regulators. President Wilson once said, "[Political] interests never unite men; interests can only divide."

We're a divided nation. On one side of the division are those who want to over-regulate our lives, and on the other side are those who want freedom under legitimate law. The battle for our country is not just about "us," *We the People*, versus "them, the House and Senate," but "us" versus *Empire Building*. Both Democrats and Republicans have built an empire of laws and regulations that now drain the life out of freedom and the free markets. Democrats scowl at the Republicans for making their rich buddies richer, while Democrats do the same thing. They both push ideologies that oppose Liberty. Each party is about keeping themselves in power. Never forget that.

Incompetent regulators and unsound monetary policies by

---

[4] William H. Peterson, *Ideas On Liberty*, The Ludwig von Mises Institute.

the Federal Reserve were the two most strategic causes of the Great Recession of 2008. What has been the response of *We the People?* We allow government's net to expand over our freedoms even more because we allow Legislators and Presidents to be both the arsonist and the fireman. The cost of this massive mistake is that the regulatory net has forced American businesses overseas by the droves.

High unemployment is always the backfiring of some previous government intervention to balance scales in society. The 2007-2008 recession is a prime example: the Federal Reserve opened the floodgates by loaning money to people they should not have loaned to in an attempt to bring about a balance in home ownership. How did that work for us?

THE BOTTOM LINE

In *The Wizard of Oz,* Dorothy was instructed to click her heels together and say, "There's no place like home. There's no place like home. There's no place like home." These magical words transported her back to the safety of Kansas, but for America there's won't be simple words that return us to constitutional accountability.

THE NEED FOR CHANGE

"Economics is concerned with what emerges, not what anyone intended,"[5] said American economist Thomas Sowell. *We the People* carry the power for change through our willingness

---

[5] Thomas Sowell, *Basic Economics: A Common Sense Guide to the Economy* (2010), Pg. 68.

to hold our representatives accountable. It is incumbent upon us to make it clear that we want an accurate representation of our views, and that might mean the sacrifice of a politician's agenda.

MY PERSPECTIVE

The 2008 political cycle was one of the most charged in recent decades. Those in Washington, D.C., whether in the Senate or Congress, responded to the financial crisis by pointing their fingers across the aisle in accusations: *That other party did it. It happened on their watch. It's the failed financial policy of their administration.*

> **Democrats and Republicans are both responsible for giving us "institutionalized greed."**

The American taxpayers deserve better than playground antics from their duly-elected representatives. Instead, they are going to be handed the bill. This violation of the public trust falls to the account of both political parties. The truth is that all on Capitol Hill are culpable in the most devastating financial nightmare since the Great Depression. Whether their sin is one of commission or omission, the collective result is the same: Democrats and Republicans are both responsible for giving us institutionalized greed.

WHAT YOU CAN DO:

- Keep your personal information from being sold to bank

affiliates by following the Privacy Rights Clearinghouse instructions found at www.PrivacyRights.org/fs/fs24-finpriv.htm
- The Federal Office of the Comptroller of the Currency helps with many banking concerns. They provide downloadable forms to file complaints against your bank at www.HelpWithMyBank.gov.

ARE YOU SAYING THAT I SHOULD NEVER USE A BANK?

Of course not. You pay your bills, make direct deposits, use your debit card, and get money orders from time to time. What I am saying—and this is especially true of the larger banks—you are not dealing with a single entity. It would be easy to be misdirected if you are not mindful of their potential motives.

HOW YOU SHOULD RELATE TO YOUR BANK:

- Use your bank. Don't let your bank use you.
- Avail yourself of their services, but don't be misled.
- Be cautious of "bait and switch" tactics.
- Remember that your information is no longer kept private.
- Keep in mind that most banks are retail brokerage houses when it comes to selling you investments.

CHAPTER THREE

CREDIT CARD COMPANIES: LEGALIZED MAFIA?

If you have integrity nothing else matters. If you don't have integrity, nothing else matters.
—Alan K. Simpson

THE ROOTS OF THE credit card trace back to 1914, when Western Union gave its preferred customers "metal money," which carried interest-free loans with deferred payments. Just 10 years later, General Petroleum Corporation issued the first metal cards for gasoline. The first plastic card was issued by American Express in 1958, and the rest is history!

WHAT DOES THIS HAVE TO DO WITH ME?

If you're a retiree then you may be tempted to skip this chapter, but *the implications of this chapter are far reaching. Irrespective of your personal credit habits, your assets are at risk if your beneficiaries carry credit card debt themselves.*

You have sacrificed, worked extra jobs, and cut corners on spending to accumulate your present nest egg. No one wants that lifetime sacrifice to be in vain. Imagine with me: your hard-earned money is passed down to your heirs, but what you don't know is that a major amount of their inheritance (what you gave them) was spent paying down their credit card debt and interest! And that is exactly what will happen unless something radical is done in Congress or by each state legislature.

> *There is enough in the world for everyone's need,
> but not enough for everyone's greed.*
>
> —Frank Buckman

In ecology, the term *predation* describes a biological interaction in which a predator kills and eats other organisms known as prey. In the financial world there is a similar interaction known as *predatory lending*. The credit card company functions as a *predator* and the consumer is its *prey*.

Predatory lending is the mother's milk of the banking and credit card industry. Predatory lenders in the credit card industry have been called legalized mafia. This lobby always seems to get its way, whether a Republican or Democrat is in office. A country that lacks integrity regarding money creates indentured servitude.[6]

---

6 If you doubt this, I encourage you to get a copy of the PBS *Frontline* program, "Secret History of the Credit Card," released November 23, 2004. http://www.pbs.org/wgbh/pages/frontline/shows/credit/

We are experiencing an artificial and manipulated 45-year low on interest rates in our country. Yet, for the first time in U.S. history, if credit card companies are based in Delaware or South Dakota then they have no legal restrictions on the interest rates they can charge. Many credit card companies charge 25-30% interest or more, making them the new "loan sharks" of America, and it is *perfectly legal*. In the card holders' agreement, credit card companies have mandatory arbitration clauses whereby the consumer (*or prey*) cannot sue them. Additionally, the *sham* legal proceedings created for arbitration, in which the outcome is essentially made in advance, are dominated by former industry lawyers. It's a fixed fight!

Nearly 150 million Americans have credit cards, totaling approximately 800 million cards in circulation. Currently, approximately 60% of Americans carry credit card balances, with the average household debt being over $15,000. Total credit card debt currently sits at approximately 900 billion dollars. From 1995 to 1999 credit card companies increased profits by 274%, from $7.3 billion to $20 billion. And, on top of that, the Federal Reserve reduced its prime rate 11 times from 9.5% in May of 2000 to 4.75% in December of 2001. *During this same time period*, the average credit card rate remained around 14% APR. The industry increased its bottom line at the expense of the consumer and continues to do so–hence the term, "legalized mafia."

> **Predatory lending is the mother's milk of the banking and credit card industry.**

The only thing that Predatory Lenders understand is the bottom line. Morality is not in their vocabulary, neither is ethics, only bottom line is profits. Greed is their heart, usury is their middle name.

–Unknown

The average American family has eight credit cards. Last year, the credit card industry made over $40 billion in profits, mostly from late payers. One bank boasted that 50% of their profits were made from fees charged to their customers. I call that indentured servitude. What would you call it?

According to www.cardwatch.com, there were nearly eight billion credit card solicitations mailed in 2006. Also in 2006, the Federal Reserve and www.cardweb.com reports the credit card debt in the United States reached a staggering $665 billion on bank cards and another $105 billion on store and gas credit cards with an average interest rate of 13.4%.

> **The new Universal Default Rule states that if you miss a payment with one creditor, all lenders have the right to change your interest rate!**

Most junk mail solicitors get your information from large direct mail companies. The top six companies sell information on about 90 million households and 140 million individuals. The odds are that you're known to all of them. By telling these companies not to sell information about you and your household, you can reduce the amount of junk mail and protect your privacy.

A LITTLE HISTORY

"In 1970 our country turned a fatal corner and debt became the engine that drove our economy. By 1980, many non-banks began to issue credit cards as well. The profits generated by these faux banks caught on and led to the megabanks we have seen in the last 20 years. Add to that the Financial Services Modernization Act of 1999, the merging of commercial banks, Wall Street investment firms and insurance companies after 1999, and you have an incestuous relationship that feeds predatory lending at a whole new level."[7]

"The fundamental contradiction in this new system is that consumers must keep the economy growing and the super-banks afloat by taking on debt. The whole point of credit cards, the way they are rendered most profitable, is that we dig ourselves into debt and stay trapped there forever. And it's hard to shop cheerfully or patriotically when we're maxed out.... By 2003 our personal debt amounted to 130 percent of our disposable income...."[8]

As a result of the deregulation laws of the 1980s and the

---

[7] Brett Williams, *Debt for Sale: A Social History of the Credit Trap*, University of Pennsylvania Press, Philadelphia, 2004.

[8] Brett Williams, *Debt for Sale: A Social History of the Credit Trap*, University of Pennsylvania Press, Philadelphia, 2004, p.3.

Financial Services Modernization Act of 1999, banks can now merge with insurance companies and Wall Street investment firms.

Citibank was more profitable than Microsoft and Wal-Mart before the 2008 crash (and afterwards it became a penny stock). They research nothing, develop nothing, design nothing, and they distribute only one thing: debt.

The worst is yet to come unless we do something about it now. We must not keep these super-banks afloat by taking on personal debt. If these banks can help us dig ourselves *into* debt and keep us there, they virtually own our lives as indentured servants!

> **If these banks can help us dig ourselves into debt and keep us there, they virtually own our lives as indentured servants!**

The primary purpose of the Office of the Comptroller of the Currency (OCC) is to regulate banks. Even though legitimate interest rates are the lowest in over 40 years Americans have *never* been so debt-ridden. Only we, as consumers, can change this. Greed goes all the way to the top and is not party specific. Ten of the largest U.S. banks control about 90% of credit card debt. They lobby powerfully in Washington on both sides of the aisle to keep their stranglehold over the American consumer.

> *Greed is a fat demon with a small mouth and whatever you feed it is never enough.*
>
> –Jan Willem Van De Wetering

Credit card companies call their cardholders who pay their entire balances by the due date "deadbeats." Those who pay only the minimum are called "revolvers." These companies remind me of the drug dealer. He says he is only helping people get what they want, for a profit. But you and I know that the consumer (drug addict) is now enslaved to the very thing that promised him freedom. Like the drug dealer, these banks search out those who will *not* be able to pay their entire balance each month. They don't like people who pay off their debt each month.

In both cases the motive is clear—addiction. The credit card company preys on addictive spending habits, but camouflages it with humorous and expensive commercials. The drug dealer preys on physiological addictions. What is the difference between the drug addict and the credit card "revolver"? One is against the law and endangers your *physical* health while the other is legal and carries the Congressional Seal of Approval, but seriously endangers your *financial* health.

Owning a credit card company is license to steal.
—Ed Mierzwinski, U.S.PIRG Program Director

Did you know that the number one complaint filed in America with the Better Business Bureau (BBB) involves abuse by credit card companies? This is staggering, considering the BBB tracks over 1,000 industries.

Credit card companies "push" their wares in a variety of

ways—through T.V. commercials, junk mail, and at retail checkout counters. And now they have gone so far as to peddle their products on college campuses and even to high school students.

> "Wealthy, powerful institutions extend expensive credit for excessive profits.... The illusion of choice and our own feelings of complicity hide the fact that debt is embodied domination, which the purpose of consumer credit is to keep you in debt in perpetuity. You are not supposed to pay interest on time or be disciplined by higher interest, penalties, fees, and harping, dunning, threats, and infantilizing phone calls.... Your credit report is accepted as an objective measure of citizenship and personal financial responsibility; it is a seamless, convenient means of reproducing inequality."[9]

Scottish philosopher David Hume said, "Avarice is the spur of industry." Avarice is an insatiable greed for riches. We need to wake up to what is happening and stop being the victims. Even though credit card debt and late payments seem a victimless crime, the top 10 issuers of credit cards admit charging 25-30% interest rates to some of their customers. They hope and *prey* you will be a late payer.

Debt is the engine driving our banking system today. Consumer debt (student loans, mortgages, and credit cards) has

---

[9] Brett Williams, *Debt for Sale: A Social History of the Credit Trap*, University of Pennsylvania Press, Philadelphia, 2004, p.6-7.

grown to over $11 trillion. Credit card lending has created a false economic boom because it is based on debt. Be assured, because of past practices by predatory lenders there will be an initial economic slowdown, followed by an additional slowdown on home purchases and other large ticket items. Unless we do something about this alarming new trend we will have another financial meltdown like the subprime mortgage lending debacle.

Liz Pulliam Weston, author, award winning nationally syndicated personal finance columnist and writer for MSNBC, says we should push to "…restore the 30 day grace period":

> "Today's 20-day grace periods all but require you to use electronic statements and online bill pay if you want to avoid late fees.... We need more breathing room. Another option, codified in the Credit Cardholders' Bill of Rights that's been introduced in Congress, would require issuers to mail statements 25 days in advance of due dates. The current minimum is 14 days."[10]

What do banks do when there is a downturn in the economy? They lower the interest rates and standards to entice more debt, which starts the cycle all over again.

Recently, the Federal Reserve Bank lowered interest rates to its Member Banks. To help the consumer, one would expect the Member Banks to also lower their rates to credit card holders. Not so. Credit card companies are converting to fixed-rates on

---

[10] Liz Pulliam Weston, "It's Time For a Credit Card Revolution," *MSN Money*, March 20, 2008.

their cards. Why? Because variable rates are tied to the prime rate, and when it falls so *should* the rate on your card. Many of these banks, in an attempt to recover from their poor lending practices (i.e., the sub-prime lending debacle), are recouping losses on the backs of credit card holders by not lowering interest rates. A fixed rate credit card is not tied to the prime rate, so the card issuer sets a fixed rate that allows them to keep a greater spread every time you use your card. Even though their cost of funds is dropping, they don't want to pass along the lower rates to you! Again, it's a fixed fight!

CREDIT CARD DEBT, LAWSUITS & STATES RIGHTS

"In a new trend for settling defaulted credit-card debt, debt buyers are filing hundreds of lawsuits each week in the Tarrant County Courthouse."[11]

"When a debtor ignores a collection lawsuit, the debt buyer wins an automatic default judgment, which can lead to garnishment suits against bank accounts and liens on nonexempt property.... You can appear in court by filing a written answer with one sentence: 'I deny the plaintiff's claim.' I tell them to show me the contract, to demonstrate that they have the authority to sue."[12]

"The states have pretty much zero authority after the Fair Credit Reporting Act and the limits on usury ceil-

---

[11] Teresa McUsic, "Unpaid Credit-Card Bills Giving Rise to Lawsuits," *Fort Worth Star-Telegram*, August 31, 2007.

[12] Jerry Jarzombek, Fort Worth attorney, as quoted by Teresa McUsic in "Unpaid Credit-Card Bills Giving Rise to Lawsuits," *Fort Worth Star-Telegram*, August 31, 2007.

ings and the limits on late fees. To be exactly precise, a credit card company is only subject to the usury limits and interest rate limits and late-fee limits *of the state where it is based.* So customers in California can't ask their state for stronger protections. They're subject to the laws of South Dakota and Delaware, and California's legislature cannot do anything about it...."[13]

SOME GOOD NEWS!

The New York state legislature passed a bill *banning* the Universal Default Rule on June 21, 2007. New York State Senator Charles J. Fuschillo, Jr. (R-Merrick) and Assemblyman Peter M. Rivera (D-Bronx) announced that both houses of legislature approved the legislation. The legislature "voted in favor of protecting New York consumers from this unscrupulous credit card practice," stated Senator Fuschillo, and Rivera agreed, saying, "This legislation sends a clear message that this type of anti-consumer behavior will not be allowed in our state anymore."

> **The truth will set you free, but first it will make you miserable.**
> -President James A. Garfield

On May 15, 2007, Senator Carl Levin (D-Michigan) and Senator Claire McCaskill (D-Missouri) introduced legislation (the Stop Unfair Practices in Credit Cards Act) following the

---

[13] Ed Mierzwinski, PBS *Frontline*, http://www.pbs.org/wgbh/pages/frontline/shows/credit/interviews/mierzwinski.html

hearing by the Permanent Subcommittee on Investigations:

> "Credit card issuers too often sock consumers with sky-high interest rates and excessive fees, making it harder and harder for families to climb out of debt.... The goal of this legislation is to put an end to unfair and abusive credit card practices that outrage so many American families. I'm afraid these practices have become too entrenched and too profitable to the credit card companies for the companies to change them on their own. Congress needs to enact pro-consumer legislation to put an end to these unfair practices."

CONSUMER RESPONSIBILITY

It is up to the consumer to bring about change. Americans need to adjust their attitude toward credit card usage. The mentality of being able to pay for something tomorrow that you cannot afford today has made us the debtor nation that we are.

Free market advocates *must* acknowledge there is an overwhelming moral hazard to usury and predatory lending. Political pressure must be put on the legislature today if we are to have a healthy America tomorrow. Let your state and federal government officials know that you and the rest of America have been harassed long enough with credit card and other usury approaches.

QUESTIONS

Are you saying credit cards are evil?

No, I have the same attitude about credit card companies that I do about banks. *Use their services, but don't let them use you.* Credit cards can protect your purchases against theft, provide discounts on airline tickets and give you insurance coverage for car rentals. They can help with discount purchases for business expenses, increase your credit score and much more. However, they can also be an albatross if you do not pay them off monthly. Merchants can still make money off fees without gorging themselves on ridiculous interest rates. Use them for leverage, but don't get sucked into their traps. Credit cards can help streamline your life considerably *if* you use them responsibly.

How do I cancel unwanted credit cards?

You should call the credit card company to verbally cancel the card and ask the company to give you a physical address (not a P.O. Box), so you can follow up with a written request to cancel. Be sure to purchase a return receipt from your post office so you can confirm they received your request to cancel.

WHAT TO DO

It's time to take control. Take a *proactive* stance regarding your personal information. Unsubscribe from credit card solicitations and other unwanted mail. Stop the flow of solicitation that daily and indiscriminately hits our mailboxes.

HERE'S HOW:

Go to www.optoutprescreen.com and stop the major credit

reporting agencies from selling your information to direct marketers or call **1-888-5-optout**. You can opt out for five years or permanently. You can always change your mind later if you wish. Make sure you do this for *every* household member if you want to maximize effectiveness.

If you want to opt out of *general sales information* that fills your mailbox each week then you can go straight to the top six companies who purchase your information. This information comes from www.junkbusters.com and is included at the end of this chapter.

Freeze your credit reports. It will cost you a little more than $30 to freeze your reports. Companies that try to view your reports to check you out will get a code telling them your reports are frozen. You can lift the freeze by notifying the bureaus and supplying them with a PIN number. Plan ahead if applying for new credit as it will take between 3 to 10 days to lift the freeze. The credit bureaus charge an additional fee to reinstate (or *thaw*) your report, although some states waive these fees for senior adults. Contact FinancialPrivacyNow.org for additional help.

Educate your children and grandchildren about the credit trap, and remember, "the debtor is slave to the lender."

Resources to Assist You

Contact the Federal Trade Commission's National Do Not Call Registry to help you get telemarketers off your back. Either call 1-888-382-1222 or visit DoNotCall.gov.

You can also add your name to the Direct Marketing Associations (DMA) file, where you can send letters and postcards (at a cost) to have your name removed from several lists with assistance on writing the letters. They also have a Deceased Do Not Contact List (DDNC). For additional information, contact them at DMAConsumers.org.

To become more knowledgeable about what you can do for yourself and your family, visit:
- www.TruthAboutCredit.org
- www.ASPIRG.org
- www.AskLizWeston.com

The Federal Trade Commission has some excellent articles designed to help the consumer. See articles "Knee Deep in Debt" (www.ftc.gov/bcp/conline/pubs/credit/kneedeep.shtm) and "How to Dispute Credit Report Errors" (www.ftc.gov/bcp/edu/pubs/consumer/credit/cre21.shtm).

Sample opt-out letters and anti-telemarketing scripts can be found at www.junkbusters.com, a very useful website to help you preserve your personal privacy. *Then write the following companies to unsubscribe:*

- Write to: Metromail Corporation
    Attn: Consumer Services
    901 West Bond
    Lincoln, NE 68521

(1-800-228-4571, Ext. 4633)

After two to three weeks, you will probably receive a postcard saying, "Thank you for notifying us of your preference," even if you sent them a *demand*, not an expression of *preference*.

- Write to: Acxiom Corporation
    Attn: Opt-outs/Consumer Advocacy
    P.O. Box 2000
    Conway, AR 72033-2000
    (1-501-342-2722)

They may send you another form to fill out. This unfairly burdens you, but *no law* stops them from making it difficult or impossible for you to stop them from making money off of your name. Acxiom (ACXM) maintains a database of about 175 million people in 110 million U.S. households, with hundreds of pieces of information available on each.

- Write to: Abacus Direct
    P.O. Box 1478
    Broomfield, CO 80038-1478
    (1-800-518-4453) or (1-303-410-5294)

Abacus runs the world's largest co-op database, where about one thousand catalogers pool information on the buying behaviors of about 88 million consumers. (Privacy advocates opposed its 1999 merger with DoubleClick.)

- Write to: InfoUSA
    Attn: Product Quality
    P.O. Box 27347
    Omaha, NE 68127
    (1-888-633-4402)

Formerly American Business Information, Inc., InfoUSA (IUSA) is the owner of ProCD, a CD-ROM containing the addresses and phone numbers of most Americans.

- Write to: Donnelly Marketing, Inc.
    Data Base Operations
    416 S. Bell
    Ames, IA 50010
    (1-515-382-5441)

After a few weeks, you will probably receive a letter acknowledging your "request" and a booklet titled Direct Marketing: Opening the Door to Opportunity, published by the DMA. Donnelly was acquired in 1999 by InfoUSA (IUSA).

- Write to: The Polk Company
    Attention: Opt-Out Coordinator
    26955 Northwestern Highway
    Southfield, MI 48034-8455
    (1-800-873-7655)

After a few weeks you will probably receive a letter stating that they have "responded to your request." Polk is privately held, but sold some of its databases to InfoUSA.

Chapter Four

Annuities: The Good, the Bad, and the Ugly

> *Some will rob you with a six-gun, and some with a fountain pen.*
>
> —Woody Guthrie

Investment, Insurance, or Rip-Off?

Identifying exploitation in the financial services industry has become my professional responsibility. Dishonesty and corruption run rampant because of the commission-based structure built into many of the products sold to senior adults. These products and their impact on seniors' investments must be scrutinized.

Many insurance companies—and the agents who represent them—want you to believe they are something more than simply life insurance agents. This is where the confusion begins. Let's identify the myths and reveal the illusions created by the insurance industry that advance deceptions about their agents and the investment opportunities they offer.

First, let's address the role of the insurance agent. Being an insurance agent is not a bad thing. In fact, it can be an honorable profession providing a valuable service. However, when an insurance agent is not satisfied with the perception that the title "insurance agent" leaves in the mind of the consumer, the challenge to be considered in a more prestigious light has produced some creative designations. If an agent is willing to participate in artful deception or misdirection, the possibilities for exploitation become endless.

> *Just like Toto in The Wizard of Oz, I want to pull back the curtain so you can see that all is not as it seems.*

In most states, insurance agents must pass an exam regulated by that state's insurance board. This license allows them to sell life and health insurance, but it also allows them to sell senior-centric products such as long-term care insurance and annuities. This license is necessary to legally sell these products, yet knowing the negative connotations associated with the insurance industry, most agents try desperately to separate themselves from the rest of the pack. They only have an insurance license, so they attempt to camouflage their lack of estate planning education and expertise behind slick company-generated presentations.

In May 2007, the Senate Special Committee on Aging, chaired by Senator Herb Kohl (D-Wisconsin), requested training materials from some insurance carriers. The committee also asked how the insurance carriers screen sales agents. In addition, they sent out similar letters to organizations that provide training or certifications related to selling products to seniors. In the letters, Senator Kohl wrote, "I am particularly troubled by companies and individuals that hold themselves out as having an expertise in senior financial matters, when in reality they have no training or very little in this extremely complicated arena."

Another primary method used by agents to give the impression of credibility to the senior population is to place a series of acronyms behind their name on business cards, such as CSA (Certified Senior Advisor). Creative designations like this bear no relationship to the education necessary to be a true Investment Advisor. These designations are not recognized by the Financial Industry Regulatory Authority (FINRA) or the Securities Exchange Commission (SEC), which are the governing bodies that oversee Financial Planners and Investment Advisors.

The course that confers the title of Certified Senior Advisor is called a "correspondence course with a multi-choice exam."[14] "'The degree is not worth the paper it is written on.... It's a scam, a way to put a title on a business card that impresses gullible seniors.'"[15] "'The training they [senior specialists] receive is often no more than marketing and selling techniques.'"[16] What

---

[14] Charles Duhigg, "For Elderly Investors, Instant Experts Abound," *The New York Times,* July 8, 2007.

[15] T. Kevin McElreath, a financial advisor from Milford, Massachusetts, as quoted by Charles Duhigg, "For Elderly Investors, Instant Experts Abound," *The New York Times,* July 8, 2007.

[16] Jack Herstein, assistant director of the Nebraska Department of Banking and Finance. (See *AARP,* May/June, 2007.)

is worse, many insurance companies actually pay for the correspondence course if the agent will agree to sell their products!

> *How many legs does a dog have if you call the tail a leg?*
> *Four, calling a tail a leg does not make it a leg.*
>
> –Abraham Lincoln

In addition to bogus designations, there are other ways that many agents will try to deceive seniors. To present himself as something he is not, an agent can pay a fee and have his picture put on the cover of an "official" looking trade publication, the inference being that he wrote the articles. On April 13, 2008, *Dateline NBC* aired "Tricks of the Trade," confirming several scams. The program exposed questionable industry practices that furnishes insurance agents with pre-published books and pre-produced radio programs featuring the agent. This intentional fraud is aimed at seniors to give the impression the agent wrote the book, or was actually interviewed on the program. This practice *screams* "Do business with me. I'm the expert." From its very inception, it is designed to mislead and lie to the senior, who sadly becomes the next potential victim. This is disinformation and fraud.

Disinformation starts with the insurance company. It then works its way out into the marketplace through agents who may have little or no integrity. Your agent may mean well, but is likely hindered by a bias, incomplete education, contests, bonuses, and sales managers. Therefore, it is up to you to be armed with the right questions and accurate information.

> *"There is no free lunch."*
> —Milton Friedman, Economist

If you attend an insurance agent's "free" lunch or dinner seminar, you will often find them reading the script to a flashy corporate-issued PowerPoint presentation. This presentation is often designed to hide the fact that they are *only* licensed to sell you annuities: an annuity becomes the answer to every investment question or dilemma. There are some insurance agents who do not participate in this blurring of reality, but in most cases an insurance agent is not qualified as an estate planner, tax planner, or an investment advisor unless they've had additional education; he is typically a salesperson marketing insurance and annuities.

ANNUITIES: THE ANSWER OR THE DILEMMA?

When you receive the insurance agent's invitation to attend a seminar, it usually contains several questions designed to invoke fear of the stock market or offer you an outrageous bonus if you move your money to him. The questions asked are carefully chosen to convince you he knows something you don't.

For example, agents promise to solve your social security tax problems or to protect you from the downside of the market, while allowing you to participate *only* in the upside. This is misleading at best. There is no "asset protection" seminar that can tell you how to hide your assets from nursing homes, solve your tax problems, prevent halitosis, cure ingrown toenails, and certainly not in the space of two hours!

When you reply to the postcard to attend one of these seminars, you have just removed yourself from their "Do Not Call List." Many times these cards will refer to a quote by AARP or have a picture of the White House on the card. Do not be fooled. This is a mass-mailer designed to get an insurance agent in front of you to sell products that could be harmful to your financial health.

Occasionally, these programs include an attorney who is usually pushing Revocable Living Trusts. His motive is to gain information regarding your assets so that his associate (an insurance agent delivering the trust) can sell you an annuity. Let's examine some of the schemes used to rob you with a pen.

Scheme #1: Pretending Patriotism

I know of an agent who begins and ends his presentations with a video depicting the war. Scenes of our soldiers overseas flash on the screen while "God Bless America" plays in the background. He is manipulating the seniors' sense of patriotism and love of country and hoping to marry their emotional response to the video with his dubious credibility. Who wouldn't want to buy from a civic-minded patriot? But first, let's ask ourselves a very logical question: What does a war film have to do with the qualifications necessary to invest your money? George Washington once said, "Guard against the *impostors* of pretended patriotism." [Emphasis mine] That statement still holds true today.

Scheme #2: Fear-Based Education

Generally, the people who hold these seminars and radio programs play on your fear and run through a maze of questions designed to frighten you. They hide the fact they are merely insurance agents whose only answer for every potential financial problem is to sell you their high commissioned, long surrender charge annuities. That is like going to a doctor for insomnia or cancer and getting the same prescription for each ailment. I would run from that doctor and question whether he earned a genuine diploma. Such is the case with many insurance agents who may earn a "degree" through mail order services or by attending a weekend seminar. They hide the fact that they are only insurance agents and that all they *really* want to sell you is an annuity.

Scheme #3: The Illusion of Credibility

Those who present business brochures identifying their membership in the Better Business Bureau, Who's Who in American Business, or even some American "ethics" organization, aim to build your confidence in them. However, they are actually directing attention *away* from the *absence* of any real financial planning credentials. Most of the letters behind their names are simply an "alphabet soup" designation that has nothing to do with financial planning.

Scheme #4: Using Religion—The Bottom Dwellers

Many of the marketing pieces used include a personal biography of the agent. Be very careful here! They will usually say *anything* that is an identifying factor with the senior population. For example, some will say things like "My family and I attend church." Many will say anything that will cause you to identify with them on a personal level. If a person's religion is real then he or she will let their life speak first. Actions speak louder than words.

"Great guy" status does not qualify anyone to manage your portfolio. *This is manipulation, pure and simple.* It does not matter if that person goes to your church, has a nice family or participates in civic organizations. If he doesn't have the proper education, credentials, and ethics, more harm could be done to your portfolio than good. And *you* have to suffer the consequences, not him.

> **"Great guy" status does not qualify anyone to manage your portfolio.**

Let me be frank with you. When people use war videos, religious words, club membership or fear of loss, let that be a warning signal to you. They *need* you to identify with them personally. They want to appear to be more than insurance salesmen. They are willing to manipulate you emotionally in order to get to your money. This is integrity fraud and ample reason for you to stay far away.

Perhaps you have been invited to a "free lunch" seminar. Most products sold at these luncheon seminars will gut you financially if you need to withdraw more than 10% of your money (10% is your fee-free withdrawal cap each year for most contracts). They make it sound like it's a real benefit that the insurance company will let you have 10% of your own money back!

What drives all of the radio shows and free lunch seminars? High commissions. Many of these annuity contracts pay 8-12% commission to the agent. High commissions are what generate the corresponding high surrender charge which could make the associated penalties extremely steep. You must carefully read the contract. This is one of the important (and dangerous) parts of the contract. You don't want to be handcuffed financially, especially in your later years. *You are officially warned!*

> *You must consider the bottom line, but make it integrity before profits.*
>
> -Dennis Waitley

Unfortunately, most people do not read the contract *before* buying the annuity. This works to the agent's advantage. The agent is aware that your knowledge is based primarily on what he has told you. Most agents only parrot their insurance training. Contracts can be very tricky things. How many of you have signed a contract to purchase something, only to find out later that you were taken advantage of? Similarly, insurance agents are rarely trained to read an annuity contract. This time it works to the advantage of both the agent and the insurance company. The insurance company knows the agent is selling only on the basis of his knowledge of the sales literature and is motivated by commissions and contests. This fosters a perfect scenario for the insurance company. This is one way they spread their disinformation.

1. **Education** is what you get when you read the small print in the contract.
2. **Experience** is what you get when you don't.

There are over 100 companies that sell indexed annuities. In fairness to those companies, not all the products are driven by agent commissions and slick presentations leading you to make ill-advised decisions. Let's evaluate these products so you can clearly see when and where they may be appropriate for you. A rule of thumb: Typically, *the simpler the product, the better it is for you!* The more complicated the product, the easier it is for the agent and insurance company to use disinformation strategies.

> **A rule of thumb: Typically, the simpler the product, the better it is for you!**

ANNUITY CLASSIFICATION

Do you remember your introduction to basic biology in junior high school? We were taught that there are two basic types of life: plants and animals. The animal kingdom can be broken down in several different ways: vertebrate or invertebrate, warm-blooded or cold-blooded, mammals or non-mammals, and so forth. In a similar manner, annuities can also be classified. All annuities fall into one of two classifications: fixed or variable. Variable annuities are investment vehicles. Therefore, your principal is at risk. These investments are typically mutual funds and bond funds placed within the annuity contracts. A securities license is required to sell variable annuities.

PART 1: VARIABLE ANNUITIES

The variable annuity is one of the most popular products sold by commission brokers. It has generated more than $2 trillion in sales. Variable annuity (VA) sales grew 16.7% in 2006, compared with 3.5% in 2005. Variable annuities are investments that are under the jurisdiction of your state and insurance commissioner as well as the Securities & Exchange Commission (SEC). The reason for this dual supervision is that your money is invested in insurance company "separate accounts" (also known as sub-accounts) in which you are purchasing mutual funds and bond funds that are tax-deferred and incur potential risk to your principal. When the insurance industry decided to market these commission-based products to senior adults, they included several costly performance enhanced options. Make an educated decision by asking the retail agent selling these products what the fees are and how they affect your overall rate of return. Or, you might want to get an impartial third party's opinion on the fees.

Sometimes retail brokers simply *switch* their clients from mutual funds in an IRA, to the same mutual funds inside a variable annuity IRA. Their motive? The commissions are much higher and they get a residual commission every year, whether they actually manage your money or not. If your broker suggests this, have him generate a report on the current mutual funds he sold you and their average returns, and compare them to the funds in the variable annuity that he wants to sell you. If his motives are less than honorable, that should be apparent when he compares the average return.

Most of the commission-driven, long-term surrender charge products create the same financial dilemma as the fixed-indexed annuity. Should you need more than 10% of your cash, you'll have to pay heavy penalties. Brokers attempt to justify switching you from funds into the Variable Annuities touting their "living benefits." However, even taking a single dollar out can potentially stop the living benefit from paying out. Why pay for a benefit that costs you dearly that also restricts your liquidity?

Wall Street Journal columnist Kelly Green makes it clear, "There are very few cases in which variable annuities make sense for retirees seeking to maximize their returns. Most financial planning specialists advise older adults to steer clear of variable annuities. The reasons? In addition to their volatility, variable annuities can create tax headaches and often carry high fees and surrender charges."

Kimberly Lankford warns to not let the bells and whistles distract you, "Although variable annuities can pay off in very limited circumstances, most investors will do better buying and holding mutual funds outside rather than inside this tax shelter."[17]

The real problem with the variable annuity is not the concept of tax deferral on the growth of mutual funds, but the complication and layers of confusion built into the product. Should you decide to purchase a commission-based variable annuity, be mindful of the surrender charges and internal fees. These can be avoided with other products.

COMMISSION OR FEE-BASED VARIABLE ANNUITY?

If you are interested in tax deferral on your money and want to have the opportunity for true market gains, why not consider a no-commission, no-surrender charge variable annuity? Let's examine the distinct differences between commission-based and fee-based variable annuities so that you are able to better evaluate which product matches your personal investment profile.

Purchasing a commission-based variable annuity generates small percentage fees for each of the multiple options available to choose. There is a fee associated for "locking in" each of the following electives:

- The highest gains for the year.
- Death benefit.
- A minimum guaranteed income upon payout.

A life insurance rider is another option that many companies offer. This provides heirs additional cash to pay taxes upon

---

[17] Kimberly Lankford, "Don't Let the Bells and Whistles Distract You," *Kiplinger*, September 1, 2005.

inheriting the money. The insurance company hopes that you will not exercise most of these options so they can capture a larger portion of your growth. With some companies, the fees associated with these electives can cost up to 3-4% of your account value each year. Scrutinize these fees to see if the commission-based product provides the best value. These fees are in addition to the management fees of the sub-accounts.

The fee-based variable annuity has no surrender charges because the agent is not paid a commission. It is called a "fee-based" variable annuity because you are actually paying an Investment Advisor to manage your account. Advantages include having more funds from which to choose and potential gains not diluted by the cost of the electives in a commission-based product. On the other hand, the guaranteed options previously listed are not available with a fee-based product. These electives could be advantageous, especially in a down market.

Companies such as Charles Schwab, Fidelity, Vanguard, and TD Ameritrade offer these products. The commissioned broker may not want you to find out this information because of the loss of huge up-front commissions and the trailer commission which are paid by some companies as well.

Many fee-based products lack the living benefit riders which commission-based agents often given as the reason for purchasing the products. Holding onto the variable annuity because of the living benefit, *even* if the current returns are horrible, is great for the company and the agent who receives renewal commissions, but terrible for the consumer who is losing value year by year.

The insurance industry's commission-based variable annuities tend to be nothing more than fear-driven products. Again, the living benefit is misrepresented as a way to shift risk onto the insurance company, yet, in most cases, it does not actually do this. This statement also holds true for most fixed-indexed annuities.

Variable Annuity Taxation

Many "financial planners" will suggest a variable annuity so that growth can be tax-deferred, especially if you are in a high tax bracket. But don't follow blindly. Under current tax laws, capital gains on mutual funds are taxed at the rate of 15% if held for one year or more. However, the same gains on the same mutual funds held within a variable annuity would be taxed as ordinary income. For example, if you are in a 30% tax bracket and place your money in a variable annuity, as you withdraw your money the interest earned is paid out first and 30% is owed in taxes. In effect, these conditions could *double* your tax liability.

Taxation to Heirs

If you own mutual funds at the time of your death, your beneficiaries will receive a stepped-up cost basis on your assets. This means that the value of the mutual funds upon your death becomes your heirs' new cost basis. As your heirs, they will owe no tax on capital gains up to $5.45 million per individual for 2016. However, if the mutual funds were held in a variable annuity, your beneficiaries would have to pay taxes on *all* the gains as ordinary income, based upon *their* tax bracket. In other words, because your mutual funds (and/or bond funds) were in an annuity, upon your death your beneficiaries do *not* get a stepped-up basis to today's value, which could be very costly when they inherit your assets.

PART 2: INDEXED ANNUITIES

On the other side of the annuity kingdom are fixed annuities. Fixed annuities are not investments. They are, by definition, savings plans because your principal is not at risk. However, in the fixed-annuity world there are many species. Some species are very simple. For example, a Single-Premium Deferred Annuity (SPDA) is available with a term as short as one year with guaranteed interest rates. This is similar to purchasing a one-year CD at your bank. The potential advantage that an annuity has over a CD is that your interest is tax deferred.

Some species in the fixed-annuity world are not as simple as the SPDA, but are complex, vague, and confusing. These are called equity-indexed annuities and are the products that are being pushed by salespeople using slogans such as "Get all of the gains of the stock market with none of the risk." They are hyped up like the Titanic, but remember, the Titanic sank.

Indexed Annuities were introduced to the United States general public in 1995. The National Association of Insurance Commissioners (NAIC) states, "An Equity-Indexed Annuity is a *fixed* annuity, either immediate or deferred, that earns interest or provides benefits that are linked to (not invested in) an external equity reference or an equity index." The NAIC goes on, "When you buy an Equity-Indexed Annuity you own an insurance contract. You're not buying shares of any stock or index."

An equity-indexed annuity is *not* an investment. It is an insurance contract that should be called a "fixed indexed annuity." From this point forward we will refer to "equity-indexed annuities" as "indexed annuities" since you don't own equity in any stock or fund.

An indexed annuity is not prone to loss of principal because your money is not in the stock market. However, it is subject to a surrender charge loss *which could actually be worse*. During the first few years, should the annuity owner need more than 10% of the annuity's current account value, he or she could be heavily penalized based on the surrender features in the contract. That could be more costly than a drop in the stock market and there is no opportunity to get the money back. These charges can be as high as 10-12% of the principal investment!

Also, indexed annuities expose the owner to inflation risks because of their historically low returns and because the money is locked up for years with surrender charges. Every inflationary cycle decreases your purchasing power when your money is eventually available penalty-free.

POTENTIAL RISKS WITH INDEXED ANNUITIES:
Surrender Charge Risk:

How long is your money inaccessible before you can get

to more than 10% of your account value? 10 years? 15 years? Longer? How long is the term? *Find out up front.*

The penalty to withdraw your money is far more severe than the penalty on a CD. With a CD you lose some of the interest, but with an annuity you could lose significant principal as well. Identify the early surrender charges in the contract before signing.

Bonus Risk

Many companies entice you with a bonus that so you will move money to them. However, they will not allow you to *keep* that bonus if you decide to move your money away from them at the end of the contract term. This feature is designed to force you to keep your money with them and annuitize it (take a monthly pay-out) at a rate specified in the contract. Again I say: *read the contract!*

The annuitized interest rate is usually 2.5% or less, sometimes guaranteed at only 1%. Additionally, some companies will *not* allow your beneficiaries to receive a lump-sum payment at your death. Your beneficiaries may have to take a five-year payout. Was this "minor" detail explained to you? Does that sound like disinformation to you?

Required Minimum Distribution (RMD)

If an IRA or 403(b) is in an annuity, be very careful when it comes time to withdraw the Required Minimum Distribution (RMD). Many insurance companies will simply send you a letter prior to your turning age 70 ½ asking IF you want to take your RMD. If you do not respond to this letter the IRS will charge a 50% penalty on the amount of the RMD. For example, if you were supposed to withdraw $5,000 but failed to do so, the IRS will penalize you $2,500. If you *assume* that your insurance agent is taking care of this for you, I have some swamp land I would like to sell you in Florida!

Interest Rate Risk

Important question: If your money is spread out in three different indexes (remember: your money is not really invested in the index, but is tied to a formula external to that index), how do you know which index or strategy to choose each year to net your best possible return?

Index Risk

There are over 40 different methods for calculating and crediting your index returns within the insurance industry. By and large, their formulas are impenetrable. It is not as simple as tying your money to an established index on a specific day and mirroring that return. Also, in the contract it states that the insurance company can change how they calculate your indexes each year. They can also change the participation rates, maximums or minimums on your caps,

Planning without action is futile; action without planning is fatal.
-President James A. Garfield

and on and on it goes. Who does this protect? The insurance companies understand the importance of keeping their flexibility. They are acutely aware of the changing market environment. This is why they put clauses in their contracts which allow them to make changes to any potential growth in your annuity balance. They do this to secure *their* profits, not yours.

CURRENT "STANDARDS" FOR ANNUITIES

Just recently the insurance industry sold $75,600,000,000 (that's 75.6 *billion* dollars) worth of fixed annuities, according to LIMRA International. A major percentage of annuities sold were fixed-indexed annuities, with virtually no clear accountability to the consumer on the previous year's average returns. If you want to know how a particular index in the securities industry has performed over the last few years, you can look online at Morningstar.com or your local newspaper. That is not the case with fixed-indexed annuities. They do not have to publish their average returns *anywhere*. Imagine that! Seventy-five billion, six hundred million dollars in new business in one year, yet there is no accountability on average returns available to the consumer. Where are the consumer advocates?

> *It is up to you to be armed with the right questions and accurate information.*
>
> ⸺ ∞ ⸺

HOW INDEXED ANNUITIES REALLY WORK

- Most of the premium dollars go to support the minimum

guarantee promised in the contract.

- A small portion of your premium is used to purchase index options.
- Your yield may change annually (or with each new indexing period) because *the participation rate* can potentially lower your gains.
- Low bond yield and high option costs may reduce the index-linked costs, therefore possibly reducing the index-linked interest rates.

If you understand the above four points then you know more than most insurance agents selling these products!

An indexed annuity allows the company the option of buying options on stocks one time annually. When an insurance company invests the dollars you give them, they take a large portion of each dollar (typically around 80%) to purchase high-quality bonds and mortgages to support the minimum guarantee promised in the contract. The remaining portion is then spent to purchase options. The price of the option determines the initial cap rate. At the end of each year, the options either expire or are cashed in if they are in the money. Then new options are purchased to hedge the index movement for the next 12 months.

Index options change daily, which causes your renewal rate caps to change as well. You only get to participate in the index growth of the options purchased (if there are any) based upon the percentage of participation in the contract. All contracts are *not* created equal. In most cases you can only change your index options once per year. For example, if you purchased an indexed annuity on August 5th, 2014 based on the Dow, which is at 16,429, then the insurance company will evaluate your account on August 5th, 2015. Should the Dow be up, you could realize a gain, *but if the index is down on that day you are credited zero.* This process is repeated each year. You are betting that on the anniversary date the index you chose will be above the preceding year. Your entire future returns are based on that one day. Who do the odds favor, you or the insurance company?

There are safety-minded people who don't want the exposure of the stock market or the flat rates of a bank, but are willing to bet on the possibility of participating in the index options from year to year. And as a vice president of Standard Insurance warns,

> "...problems can occur if the broker creates an expectation in the client that the renewal rate cap is directly linked to the index performance. This is an unrealistic expectation. It's quite possible the renewal rate cap will go down even when the index is going up. On the flip side, the client may be happy to know the same holds true when the index is going down–it's quite possible in that scenario that the renewal rate cap could go up."[18]

---

[18] James E. Teague, "Index Annuity Renewal Rate Caps: What Goes On Behind-The-Scenes," *National Underwriter Life & Health*, August 5, 2007.

Possible Legislation

The Securities and Exchange Commission (SEC) has proposed under Rule 151A, that indexed annuities be registered with the SEC under the Securities Act of 1933 (the Securities Act). The powers that be continue to vacillate. However, transparency would force these products to prove their actual average return, so that consumers truly know what they are purchasing.

Legal Action

Minnesota Attorney General Lori Swanson filed suit against such insurance industry giants as Allianz, Midland National, and AmerUs Life, now part of the Aviva USA Corporation. She warns,

"Beware high-pressure sales tactics and seminars. Some unscrupulous sellers use high-pressure sales pitches, seminars and telemarketing. Beware of agents who 'cold call' you, contact you repeatedly, offer 'limited time offers,' show up without an appointment, or won't meet with you if your family is present. Beware of estate planning 'seminars' that are actually designed to sell annuities. Beware of seminars that offer free meals or gifts. In the end, they are rarely free. Beware of agents who give themselves fake titles to enhance their credibility."

"Be on guard against 'bonuses'. Agents and insurance companies may offer bonuses to entice investors, such as additional interest points on their return. The benefits of such 'bonuses' are often outweighed by increased fees and administrative costs to the investor. Bonuses may be simply marketing gimmicks."[19]

REAL ACCOUNT VERSUS PHANTOM ACCOUNT

Not only are agents offering bonuses, but also one of the newer products adds to their bonus a 7.2% guaranteed account if you purchase their additional income rider. The sales pitch is that your money is *guaranteed* to double every ten years. Don't be fooled by this trickery. There are two accounts, a *reality account* and an *income account* (or what I call *a phantom account*).

The *reality account* is based upon the index options that you choose and their performance. When you are eligible to draw on the *income account* then they usually only allow you to draw out a percentage of the account annually. The contract owner will have to withdraw these monies for about 20 years just to get back the money originally given to the insurance company! This means that the investor never realizes the increase in the income account. The heirs *only* receive the reality account *less* all the disbursements from the income account at your demise. So did you ever really own the *income account*? No, it was a *phantom account* that led you to believe you had more money than you actually had. The insurance companies that sell these products refuse to be plain and simple with the consumer regarding real returns on their money. This is one of the reasons why they have come under scrutiny by the Securities & Exchange Commission and

---

[19] Lori Swanson, "Annuities: Beware of Unsuitable Investments for Seniors." See http://www.ag.state.mn.us/consumer/Publications/AnnuitiesUnsuitableInvforSeniors.asp

face numerous lawsuits by Attorney General Offices all across the country. However, due to the strong political powers of the insurance industry, sales of these deceptive products continue.

QUESTIONS TO ASK YOURSELF:

- Why am I giving my money to an insurance agent to assist me with my choices of indexes when he usually does not have a securities license, which is required in the investment world?
- Is this money I can afford to "forget about"? (Long-term surrender charges may apply.)
- Is this money "stuck"? Have I lost all flexibility to move the money to different sectors as the markets change?
- Why am I depending on an insurance agent to annually choose the indexes of securities-based investments, like the Russell 2000, Lehman Brothers bonds, the Dow and the S&P 500, of which he very likely knows nothing about? *That is the ten million dollar question!*

QUESTIONS TO ASK THE AGENT:

- What are the annual administrative or asset fees? Are these fees deducted from my interest every year? If the agent is not really "managing" my money, why are they charging these fees? (This question should be asked about any financial product that you consider purchasing.)
- Can the company, at its own discretion, lower the cap to limit the amount of interest I can earn each year? Why

would they do this?
- Can the company lower my participation rate in an index from year to year?
- If I spread my money out in three indexes, and two of them do not grow, do I get credited *zero* on those dollars? For example, you have $90,000 and place $30,000 in three different indexes. If two of those indexes get credited zero because of market influences, the third index would have to earn a 9% return for you to receive an overall return of 3% on your money that year.
- Does the company have a history of changing the participation rates and caps? How can I obtain that information?
- What is the historical performance of the annuity with the index you chose? Hint: There isn't one! (Unlike the securities world).

This is a bit more complex than it was presented to you, isn't it? The next time you hear your local financial pundit say, "Lock in all the stock market gains with no risk to your principal," *tune your radio to another station*! That "financial expert" is one taco short of a combination plate, or you are listening to a charlatan.

> *"Planning without action is futile; action without planning is fatal."*
>
> -Anonymous

Many agents selling fixed-indexed annuities play on your

fear of the stock market. They exaggerate the benefits of their favorite product. The product that is best for you is often determined by some bonus program or incentive trip, again at your expense. If you aren't equipped to understand the truth, you become their next victim.

There are only a handful of companies that offer well-designed, consumer-oriented contracts. Look for companies that publish their renewal rate caps each month and offer bailout options without surrender charges. *Hint: those products pay lower commissions!*

If you are still considering purchasing an annuity, keep the following in mind:

- Review the surrender charges.
- The minimum rate guarantee often does not apply to 100% of your entire principal.
- You have limited liquidity. Withdrawals beyond 10% lose principal.
- Review the participation rate, the cap rate, the spread (there is a difference on what you get off the index option and what the company keeps) and your index options before signing the contract.
- Dividends are typically not included when calculating your index-linked earnings.
- The time value of money: the value of your money is eroding as inflation increases.

If you desire to purchase an indexed annuity, buy one with

a short-term surrender charge that will allow you to evaluate the performance. Consider purchasing it from a securities-licensed agent who has the business and market acumen to appraise the market conditions and adjust the indexes from year to year as necessary.

The Bottom Line

Ask yourself this question: If an indexed annuity is the "be-all, end-all" vehicle for large sums of money, then why aren't the insurance companies willing to publish the average rate of return on the indexed products they sell? Even the advertised rate of return is for an income rider, not for the actual cash value of the account. Reporting *actual* returns is a requirement that the Securities & Exchange Commission places on all securities firms. Insurance companies have managed to insulate themselves from this type of scrutiny. I think it is time for them to become accountable. What do you think?

Question

Are you saying all insurance agents are not to be trusted?

No. I'm saying you need to properly assess what you are buying before you sign on the dotted line. Don't base your decision solely upon the agent's influence, opinion, or product knowledge. Read the contract! This is your money, not the agent's.

CHAPTER FIVE

LIFE SETTLEMENTS VS. VIATICALS AS AN INVESTMENT

LIKE A HOME OR other personal property, life insurance policies are a financial asset and can provide financial stability for those who have been diagnosed with a life-limiting illness. Many times, however, those insured desire to settle their affairs prior to their passing. They have the option to sell their asset (life insurance policy) in the viatical market.

Many clients over the years have called and asked me the difference between a Life Settlement and a Viatical. The difference, from an investment perspective, can be costly. With a life settlement you are typically purchasing a partial ownership in a life insurance policy that has been sold in the open market. The insured person may or may not have major health issues, which makes the life settlement a potentially long-term investment.

Another downside of a life settlement is that life expectancies can be miscalculated by the provider of the policy. If this is the case, you may have to pay additional premiums for the policy when they come due, thereby decreasing your overall return. This is very important. Unless the provider of the policy is using multiple, reputable outside firms that study life expectancies (LE), you could even pay annual policy premiums, which can create a negative return on your investment.

Another negative to life settlements is that science is continually evolving and cures for minor illnesses are often just around the corner. In other words, the person whose policy you are purchasing may out live you!

A viatical settlement, on the other hand, is the sale of a life insurance policy by a person with a confirmed, shortened life expectancy. He or she sells the policy to a third party for an amount less than its face value. The amount that is paid to purchase the policy varies based upon the individual's life expectancy and the estimated premiums needed to carry the policy until the passing of the insured.

Viatical policies can be a far superior investment to a regular life settlement, assuming you are purchasing a policy where the client has brain cancer, pancreatic cancer or Lou Gehrig's disease. All of these diseases add some predictability to the life expectancy of the policy that you are purchasing. If you are considering purchasing a viatical (Latin for *help along a difficult journey*), you still need a reputable outside firm to substantiate your conclusions on whether this is a good/safe investment choice for you.

Whether you choose a life settlement or a viatical, multiple independent life expectancies should be obtained by the carrier. This ensures optimal control of each case and that the fairest price is paid for each viatical or life settlement. Thorough underwriting, superior administration and the ability of the carrier to obtain periodic health statements from doctors are paramount.

In the U.S. approximately 1.4 million people will be diagnosed and over 500,000 people will die from cancer each year. If you use a firm that eliminates brokers and buys directly from the public, you will potentially enhance the overall return on your investment.

A life expectancy of less than 5 years with a viatical policy may be a great investment, especially if you purchase it through your IRA. Taxes are not payable until you begin your distribution phase of the IRA, April 1st after the year you turn 70.5 years old. If you are the owner of a Roth IRA and you have held it for over 5 years, the viatical investment could be right down your alley. As the investment grows with potential double-digit returns, all the growth is tax free when withdrawn. Some people think the idea of purchasing a policy, just waiting for that person to die is morbid. If you cannot identify with the genuine relief your investment offers to a terminally-ill patient, then a viatical or a life settlement is not the investment for you! However, if you identify that policy as just another investment, like a car or a home that people can own and sell, this may be an appropriate investment for your portfolio.

CHAPTER SIX

How to Protect Yourself from Identity Theft Without It Costing You an Arm and a Leg

IDENTITY THEFT HAS PARALLELED the growth and expansion of the internet. With personal information floating freely, retirees are becoming major targets for internet fraud. An entire protection industry has grown out of the need to protect and educate the consumer and his personal information. One of these firms is called Investor Protection Trust which specializes in elder investment protection. One can also go to www.eldercare.gov or call 1-800-677-1116 (adult protective services) if you suspect financial fraud.

According to Eversafe, (www.eversafe.com) retirees lose more than $2.9 billion per year by not being protected. Eversafe offers a monthly scanning service to protect against the possibility of fraudulent activity. There are even new applications for iPhones like BillGuard. This application has a money tracker that will coincide with other forms of credit/debit card protection.

If you are retired and do not plan on using credit in the future, there are some simple things you can do. If you want to opt out of pre-approved credit card offers, you can call 888-567-8688. Also, you can place a security freeze on your credit reports by contacting Equifax, TransUnion, and Experian. This prevents companies from looking at your credit report (except those with whom you already have a financial relationship).

IdentityGUARD, MetLife Defender, and Lifelock, among others, will protect your identity for a monthly fee. You can also find technology training through Older Adults Technology Services (www.oats.org), which helps seniors stay safe while online. OATS serves as a model for programs all across the nation on safety tips while surfing the net.

Identity security is not exclusively applied to technology. Below are a few things you can do offline to help your information stay secure:
- Always shred any document with personal information before discarding
- Never give personal information to anyone with whom you do not have a prior relationship
- Never use personal information to create passwords
- Change passwords regularly, but keep a master listed tucked away somewhere very safe.
- Keep a copy of all credit cards both front and back. This

way you will know the card information to cancel if it is ever lost or stolen.

Whatever your choice, whether young or old, you need to protect your bank accounts, credit cards, and social security numbers as well as those of your loved ones. Take action and gain peace of mind!

CHAPTER SEVEN

REVERSE MORTGAGES: BUYER BEWARE

Truth fears no questions.

–Unknown

YOU'VE PROBABLY SEEN THE commercials on TV about Reverse Mortgages. Spokesmen actors such as Henry Winkler, Robert Wagner, and Pat Boone are featured advocates for Reverse Mortgages. They are paid to market a fairly old concept which has recently resurfaced in ads aimed at senior adults. Reverse Mortgages can be a feasible answer to a difficult question for some people. However, they are not a "one size fits all" solution. A Reverse Mortgage can be an expensive venture in an attempt to access your cash and is fraught with multiple restrictions and fees.

What is a Reverse Mortgage?

A Reverse Mortgage is a loan against the equity in your home that does not have to be paid back for as long as you live in your home. It is a way for homeowners, age 62 and older, to turn part of their home equity into usable cash.

Selling Points of a Reverse Mortgage:
- You retain full ownership of your home.
- The home *must* be your principal residence.
- You may live in your home as long as you wish.
- The cash received is tax free, therefore does not affect Social Security or Medicare.
- No monthly repayments are required.
- There isn't any income or credit qualifying.
- Only the home is liable for the loan. In other words, no liability can pass to your heirs.
- There isn't any prepayment penalty should you decide to pay back the loan.
- The older the borrower, the more money you can access. The amount loaned to a couple is based on the age of the *younger* borrow.

Buyer Alert: If one spouse is under the age of 62, *that* spouse must be removed from the title and waive homestead rights. If the spouse desires to be reinstated with homestead rights (once he or she reaches age 62), the loan will have to be refinanced at a cost of approximately 5% of the appraised value of the house.

WHO PROVIDES REVERSE MORTGAGES?

The primary lender for reverse mortgages is the Home Equity Conversion Mortgage (HECM), which first became available in 1989. The Federal Housing Administration (FHA) insures the HECM as part of the U.S. Department of Housing and Urban Development (HUD). Conventional Reverse Mortgage Loans are not insured by the federal government, but they feature most of the same important consumer protections. Reverse Mortgages are on the rise, according to the National Reverse Mortgage Lenders Association which reported that there were 107,558 reverse mortgage loans processed in 2007, compared to only 6,640 in 2000.

How to Identify Consumer-Friendly Lenders:

- A good lender can explain your loan in everyday language.
- A good lender won't pressure you.
- A good lender will explain the costs.
- A good lender will honor their commitments.
- A good lender will advise you that if you live on a fixed income and have trouble paying property taxes or homeowners insurance you could be forced into foreclosure.
- A good lender will let you decide how you access your cash.
- A good lender will let you know which options you have and explore these options with you.
- A good lender makes you feel informed and confident.

How much can I borrow on my home with a Reverse Mortgage?

On an FHA-insured HECM, there is a formula which includes the age of the borrower(s) and the appraised value of the property. There are maximum loan limits based on your city and county. The current 2008 HUD lending value limit is $200,160. If your home exceeds the FHA limits, you could apply for a Fannie Mae Home Keeper Loan.

The April 2008 *Consumer Report Money Adviser* states that the lending formula for a Reverse Mortgage is drawn from actuarial and compound-interest tables. The article goes on to state, "The HUD estimates that on a loan with a 9% interest rate, a 65-year-old could borrow about 22% of the home's value, a 75-year-old up to 41%, and an 85-year-old about 58%."

How Are Interest Rates Determined?

The interest rates on a Reverse Mortgage Loan are set by the federal government each Tuesday. All loans are Accelerated Rate Mortgages (ARMs) unless the loan is considered a Jumbo Loan of $417, 000 or more, in which case you have a fixed rate that is set two days before closing. All ARMs are tied to the 1-year T-Bill plus 1.75%, with a ceiling interest rate on your loan of 10%. The FHA offers two adjustable rates: a monthly and an annual. You can "lock-in" your interest rate for up to 60 days.

The FHA is working on expanding the current maximum lending limit available to range from $200,162 to $362,790. Fannie Mae Home Keeper Loans, otherwise known as Conventional

Loans, are currently available and start at $417,000. Because Home Keeper Loans do not carry Mortgage Insurance Protection (MIP), their interest rates can be considerably higher; however, conventional programs typically offer lower upfront costs, especially if you take a lump-sum. Conventional loan interest rates are typically based on the London Interbank Offered Rate (LIBOR), plus a margin with adjustable and fixed rates. You can also qualify for the lesser of either:

A Reverse Mortgage can be an expensive venture in an attempt to access your cash and is fraught with multiple restrictions and fees.

1). The appraised value or the HECM (home equity conversion mortgage) FHA mortgage limit of $625,500.

2). The actual sales price of the house.

WHAT ARE SOME COSTS ASSOCIATED WITH PURCHASING A REVERSE MORTGAGE?

There is much to consider before applying for a Reverse Mortgage. It is imperative to *shop fees and closing costs*, because this is where your pocketbook gets hit the hardest. Do your homework regarding these expenses before meeting with a qualified counselor *or* lender. Be aware of the following fees and expenses:

- **Origination fee** – A charge, typically 2% of the loan, which covers the lender's operating expenses and agent commissions.

- **Mortgage Insurance Premium (MIP)** – A 2% charge which protects the government in the event your loan servicing company goes out of business. You will also owe 0.5% of the loan balance in mortgage insurance premiums every year.
- **Appraisal fee** – Pays for appraisers, who assign a current market value on your home for loan purposes and who also check for structural integrity.
- **Closing costs** – Includes credit report, escrow, flood certification, document preparation, recording fee, courier fee, title insurance, pest inspection, survey and more.
- **Loan service fee** – This could range from $30-40 *per month*!

Don't lock yourself in with one representative. Shop your costs just as you would any other major purchase or loan. You will be amazed at how the fees vary, and you do not want to end up overpaying.

How Do I Access the Cash with a Reverse Mortgage?

- All at once, in a single lump sum.
- A periodic cash advance, such as monthly.
- As a "credit line" account that lets you decide when and how much cash you receive. This leaves the balance to

grow at an interest rate equal to the loan rate. (About 70% of the people take their money this way.)
- A combination of these payment methods.

When Do I Have to Pay the Money Back?
- If the home is sold.
- After the death of the last borrower.
- When no borrower has lived in the home for 12 months. (The mortgage lender sends a letter each year confirming that the home is still your primary residence.)
- If taxes and homeowners insurance become delinquent.
- If the home is not properly maintained. Each lender has their own criteria for property maintenance and a system in place for oversight. You may have to provide answers on an annual questionnaire regarding changes or additions to the property, such as painting, fencing, landscaping, etc.

Don't lock yourself in with one representative. Shop your costs just as you would any other major purchase or loan.

Traditional Mortgage vs. Reverse Mortgage

Purchasing Your Mortgage	Reversing Your Mortgage
Making payments	Receiving payments
Purchasing a home	Accessing cash in your home
Debt decreases	Debt increases
Home equity increases	Home equity decreases

WHAT ARE SOME NEGATIVE POINTS OF A REVERSE MORTGAGE?

One touted benefit of Reverse Mortgages is that payments received are not taxed as ordinary income. Consequently, it does not increase taxation on your Social Security. What Reverse Mortgage salesmen conveniently leave out is that you are simply getting back your *own* money. *This* is why there is no taxation!

However, a drawback to Reverse Mortgages is that the payments received are considered a liquid asset. This additional income could potentially disqualify you for Medicaid, Supplemental Security Income, or other public aid.

As pointed out in *Consumer Report Money Adviser*, beware of brokers and insurance agents who want you to purchase a Reverse Mortgage so that they can sell you an annuity or a life insurance product. If you use the money to purchase an annuity, you are likely facing huge, long-term surrender charges with limited access to your money. If you put the money into a life insurance policy, there may be virtually *no* recourse to access your money should you need it.

These negative aspects are a few of the reasons why meeting with a qualified HUD counselor is necessary. HUD has a network of housing and counseling agencies; both public and non-profits are approved by the Federal Government to provide this service.

Make sure that your counselor uses AARP's model specifications. Some of the counselors are actually *paid by the lenders*. According to an article in *Consumer Report Money Adviser* titled "Watch Out for Sneaky Sales Tactics," high-pressure sales tactics are a growing concern. The article quotes a spokesperson for CEASE, the Coalition to End Elder Financial Abuse, in testimony before the Senate Special Committee on Aging in December 2007:

A Reverse Mortgage payment could be counted as liquid assets and potentially disquality you from Medicaid or other public aid.

"We are now seeing insurance broker's actively recruiting insurance agents to promote reverse mortgages at senior centers.... Some brokers are even offering to help insurance agents become HUD-certified counselors. They are instructing the agents that they can ethically get the senior to pull out home equity in order to buy insurance products."

REVERSE MORTGAGES: BUYER BEWARE | 89

What Are Some Potential Factors that Could Jeopardize the Status of Your Reverse Mortgage Loan?

Renting all or part of your home could disqualify you.

Adding a new owner to the title of your home (special warranty deeds or trusts) is not permitted.

Changing your home's zoning classification could affect your loan.

You cannot take a second mortgage against your home.

Long-term stay in a nursing home (1 year) could accelerate your loan repayment.

Buyer Alert!

When purchasing a Reverse Mortgage, you have a predetermined (HUD) amount of money available which is based upon the age of the youngest borrower. The remaining equity is inaccessible to you and could virtually become the property of the lending institution. This dilemma occurs because the homeowner's property value does not typically accelerate fast enough to offset the reverse mortgage expenses. Your remaining equity is being "devoured" to satisfy the conditions of the Reverse Mortgage Loan. The only recourse to access your "unavailable" equity is to sell your home, or repay the entire loan.

> *One alternative to obtaining a Reverse Mortgage is a Home Equity Loan.*

ARE THERE ALTERNATIVES TO THIS TYPE OF LOAN?

One alternative to obtaining a Reverse Mortgage is a Home Equity Loan. Consider the costs and fees associated with a Reverse Mortgage and a Home Equity loan:

Reverse Mortgage vs. Home Equity Loan

Has approx. $30-40 per month administration fee	Little or no ongoing administration fees
Adjustable rate can go up to 10% by federal law, unless you purchase a fixed-rate loan	Interest rate is fixed and can be written off on tax return
Mortgage Insurance Premium (MIP) is 2% at origination and 0.5% is added each year on the unpaid balance	No charges
If you go into a nursing home, note will be due and payable after the first year	No negatives if you enter a nursing home as long as payments are made
No monthly payment	Usually a monthly repayment

Many Reverse Mortgage Loans are Accelerated-Rate Mortgages (ARM). These tend to be more costly than traditional loans because they are "rising debt" loans. The interest is added to the principal loan balance each month, which causes the total amount of the interest owed to increase significantly as the interest compounds. Ask your lender what the total amount loan cost (TALC) rate is. The TALC rate is the projected annual average cost of the Reverse Mortgage and includes all the itemized costs.

Have a knowledgeable, trusted friend help you examine the contract for acceleration clauses or the lender's potential to share in equity appreciation. It would be a good idea to get a consensus among your heirs that a Reverse Mortgage is the best way to help you access the additional cash you may need.

What Are the Alternatives If I Need Additional Cash or Income?

- Purchase a home equity loan. There are many advantages with this option, especially with interest rates being at historic lows. However, remember that when you apply for a home equity loan, you have to qualify and your fixed interest rate could be 1.5% to 2% higher than a 30-year mortgage. Call your local bank or visit www.FinancialFreedom.com.
- Open a Home Equity Line of Credit (HELOC). It operates like a credit card with a revolving balance and a variable rate. You can withdraw money as you need it

and pay only the accrued interest each month. Be aware of balloon payments and prepayment penalties. This loan is usually 10 to 15 years.

- Take out a convertible loan, which is a hybrid between the traditional home equity loan and the home equity line of credit. In essence you have two loans, one with variable rates from which only the interest is due and a second with a fixed rate where interest and principal is due each month.
- Consider a Property Tax Deferral on your home. Contact your local county tax assessor's office to determine your interest rate. It is usually simple interest, not compounded. Not having to write that check each year might be all the additional cash you need to be financially comfortable.
- Look into Reverse Mortgages offered by local and state governments. These loans are usually limited to those with low to moderate incomes. And unlike a Home Equity Mortgage Loan, you are restricted as to what you can do with the proceeds.
- Create your own Reverse Mortgage with your family or friends. Set up a line of credit secured by your home, which could possibly save you money on closing costs and monthly fees.
- Sell your property. You can then rent or buy less expensive property and invest the difference. This could simplify your lifestyle and, if your current home is older

with potential problems, moving could save you money and headaches.

- Visit the AARP website to review other options and additional ideas. Use the AARP calculator at www.rmaarp.com to estimate your costs.

WARNING:

Reverse Mortgage companies are now sending out the same marketing propaganda that credit card companies are using. Be wary of letters that say "pre-selected" or "you are now eligible to stop making mortgage payments immediately." These companies are financial predators. Sometimes, they even display the Better Business Bureau insignia on their brochure in an effort to appear trustworthy. Simply place the brochure in your shredder. Don't give them the time of day.

> *Be wary of letters that say "pre-selected" or "you are now eligible to stop making mortgage payments immediately."*

U.S. SENATE SPECIAL COMMITTEE ON AGING

On December 12, 2007 Committee Chairperson Senator McCaskill stated before the committee:

"We have gone through a savings and loan collapse, a stock-market bubble, and are currently in the middle of a lending mess [Sub-prime mortgages]. Our goal is to make sure that reverse mortgages don't become the scandal of the next decade."

Congress is looking into creating a suitability test for seniors who are considering a Reverse Mortgage to protect them from unscrupulous mortgage lenders.

QUESTION
Can a Reverse Mortgage ever be a good choice for a retiree?

Yes, but *only* if:
- You are living on social security with overhead (debts and property taxes) that is more than you can afford.
- You have no heirs, or the home is not important to your heirs.
- Staying in your current home is the most important thing to you at this time *and* there are no other options to meet this objective.

CHAPTER EIGHT

LONG-TERM CARE: IS IT RIGHT FOR ME?

Life is filled with golden opportunities carefully disguised as irresolvable problems.

—John Gardner, former Secretary of State

THE COMIC STRIP "THE Wizard of ID" had a recent column fitting this topic. It is the story of a man who comes to the Wizard and says, "I had a dream that I was in a room where women outnumbered men ten to one. What could it mean?" The Wizard, in his comical way, yet with measured precision, says, "You were either in a quilting bee or in a nursing home."

Of course this is meant to be humorous, but a recent U.S. Census predicts that by 2030 almost one out of five Americans, about 72 million people, will be age 65 or older. Baby boomers moving into the retirement brackets has caused health care issues, and their spiraling costs, to become a national concern.

This chapter will explain what Medicare is and how it relates to Long-term Care coverage. It will also look at the history of Medicare and help clear up any confusion about what Medicare covers as opposed to what Long-term Care covers.

WHAT IS MEDICARE?

The federal government introduced health insurance into Congress in 1935. Ten years later, President Harry S. Truman endorsed a National Health Bill. In 1961, President John F. Kennedy asked Congress to recommend a health insurance program for the elderly, using social security as its base for financial support. In 1965, President Lyndon B. Johnson signed Medicare into law. Numerous Medicare changes were made from 1972 to 1997. And in 2003, President George W. Bush signed the Medicare Modernization Act. By 2006, both Medicare Part D, which covers outpatient drug benefits, and the Deficit Reduction Act regarding changes in Medicaid eligibility, became realities.

Medicare is a federal insurance program for people age 65 and over and for individuals with disabilities. For those 65 and over, Part A covers hospital bills (or the majority), and Medicare Part B covers doctor bills (or the majority). Part B is paid for out of a portion of your Social Security check each month. Some people choose to give their social security payment to a Health Maintenance Organization (HMO); others choose to purchase a Medicare supplement. Medicare supplements, also known as Medigap insurance, cover the "gaps" that original Medicare does not cover. It is not Long-term Care; it simply *coordinates* with Medicare by covering co-pays and deductibles.

What Medicare Insurance Covers:
- Doctors and hospital expenses for 10 to 31 days with a maximum of 100 days.
- Limited benefits for short-term nursing home stay.

Requirements for short-term nursing home care:
1. You must be in a skilled nursing home facility.
2. You must have a previous hospital stay of at least three days.
3. You must be medically benefiting from the stay for rehabilitation purposes.

MEDICARE AND LONG-TERM CARE ARE *NOT* THE SAME THING!

Long-term Care Insurance (LTC) is a risk protection tool. Many people don't consider the risk to be worth spending the money, while others believe that everyone *must* have LTC. In this section we will discuss the "true" statistics regarding nursing home care and other related services.

We don't really know how or when we will have a health issue. LTC provides a back-up plan to cover our needs and protect the assets that we spent a lifetime accumulating.

The aging of America's population has given LTC a whole new meaning. Remember, just a few years ago, nursing homes were few and far between, and many were only in small towns. Today, we see

> *Long-term Care Insurance is a risk protection tool.*

independent living, assisted living and nursing home facilities in almost every neighborhood.

Long-term care has grown to a complex formal network that includes medical, nursing, social, and other related services. The average monthly institutional cost in our country is $6,250. With that in mind, think about this:

- There are more than 1.9 million nursing home residents in the U.S.
- There are approximately one million individuals living in assisted living facilities.
- Almost 200,000 individuals are receiving care at adult day care centers.
- Nearly 1.5 million people receive home health care services.
- 745,000 people (average age of 78) live in continuing-care retirement communities.

(From www.aahsa.org, AAHSA: Aging Services: The Facts 3/14/07)

The number of Americans turning age 65 jumped from 6,000 per day in 2007 to 10,000 per day in 2011. Exponential numbers are just around the corner. According to the *2012 US Census*, 80 million people—that's roughly one in five Americans—will be termed *elderly* in the year 2030. This is simply *staggering*!

Satchel Page, the great baseball player of yesteryear once said, "Age is a question of mind over matter; if you don't mind, it doesn't matter." With the increasing number of seniors today that are diagnosed with some type of dementia and in need of care, it does matter.

Now, having said all that, I want to clarify some of the myths and facts concerning Long-term Care Insurance. Remember, LTC is a risk protection tool.

Long-term care has grown to a complex formula network that includes medical, nursing, social and other related services.

1. **Myth** – You need to buy long-term care when you are young because more than 40% of people who need LTC are under age 65.

   Fact – 238 million people between the ages of 18-64 receive health care assistance. Only 159,000, or less than 1%, receive nursing home care.

2. **Myth** – Medicare will pay for your LTC expenses if you are over age 65.

   Fact – Medicare only pays for short-term skilled care in nursing facilities and limited skilled care at home. It is not a long-term care policy.

3. **Myth** – There is nearly a 50% chance that a person will require 24-hour care in a nursing home facility.

   Fact – Only 1% of those aged 65-74 live in a nursing home. Only 4% of those ages 75-84 and 19% of those 85 years and older are currently living in a nursing home.

4. **Myth** – If you purchase LTC at age 65 you probably don't need inflation protection.

Fact – The average age of admission into a nursing home is 83. If you are age 65 today, you have 18 more years of inflation and need to consider that the average stay in a nursing home for a senior adult is 2.8-3.2 years.

More facts to consider:
- Women face a greater possibility of needing long-term care. They tend to outlive their spouse.
- Most long-term care costs are paid for by the income and assets of individuals and their families. Most people still have family members who provide in-home care and act as unpaid caregivers. They help with the basic activities for daily living such as bathing, dressing, eating, restrooms, medications, and grooming.
- If a person needs LTC and has few assets and income, Medicaid can be one option. Medicaid is a federal and state government program that acts like a safety net when individuals qualify because of minimal assets (usually $2000) and income (check with your state Medicaid offices). President Bush signed the Deficit Reduction Act (DRA) on February 8, 2006 which changed the Medicaid asset transfer rules and penalty period.

If you have a spouse, friend or relative who is in need of nursing home care, you can visit the Consumers Union Center for Consumer Health Choices website at ConsumersUnion.org.

Insurance Poor!

I'm sure you are familiar with the term "insurance poor." You cannot purchase a kitchen appliance, office furniture or a car without being offered an extended warranty! (Insurance!) We even keep home owners insurance after our homes are paid for. The reason we do this is because we are afraid our home might burn down. Now what is the likelihood of our house burning down? Not that great, but we still carry the insurance *just in case*!

> **Do not be manipulated by agents who use misleading statistics to create fear in an effort to sell you a LTC policy.**

Everyone needs to evaluate their own personal situation in order to decide:

- What genetic factors will contribute to long-term care need.
- If the premiums are affordable.
- What value you place on independence.
- If there are other housing/care options available to you (family/friends).

Do not be manipulated by agents who use misleading statistics to create fear in an effort to sell you a LTC policy.

How Do I Choose a Long Term Care Policy?

If your situation dictates the need for LTC, every state has a nursing home guide that discusses the types of policies that are available for you to purchase. They are published by the insurance division of your state. When looking to purchase LTC, you should look for a company that has superior ratings with companies like A.M. Best, Moody, and Standard & Poor. You want to look for policies where these items are covered:

- Adult day care
- Bed reservations clause
- Case management
- Spousal discount
- Respite care
- Inflation-rider options
- Premiums that are rarely increased

All are very important questions that need to be answered when reviewing LTC policies. A good rule of thumb is that your premiums for LTC should not exceed 15% of your income (Remember: the company can increase those premiums over time).

Make sure that you understand all the options and the length of time you are covered on the policy. If your spouse is already deceased and you are willing to give the nursing home your social security check and your pension check, you may only need a policy that covers $50 per day. As an example, suppose you need $150 per day coverage or $4500 a month. If your pension and social security equals $3000 a month, that covers $100 per day. So all you need is a $50 per day policy to make up the difference. Do not be oversold on what your actual needs are.

If this is a subject that you have not broached with family members, you can go to the University of Minnesota Extension Services and get a copy of their excellent article, "Breaking the Silence: Initiating Family Conversations About Financing Long-Term Care." Or you might want to go to the U.S Department of Health & Human Services website at http://longtermcare.gov and review the types of services and costs, as well as an overall education of what help you will need when discussing these decisions with family members.

OTHER LONG TERM CARE OPTIONS

LTC coverage, as a hybrid product, can now be purchased through life insurance policies, annuity contracts and other vehicles. You are actually purchasing an annuity or life insurance that is linked to long-term care coverage, but you do still have to qualify for the coverage. The advantage of a life insurance policy or an annuity is that your family always gets back a benefit. However, with a traditional LTC policy, should you die in your sleep before entering a nursing home, there's no asset to pass on to your heirs with most policies. Whatever you choose, make sure that you review your options just as you would any important purchase.

Whatever you choose, make sure that you review your options just as you would any important purchase.

Here are some services that can help you choose the right facility for your family or loved one:

- Leading Age (formerly, American Association of Homes & Services)
    Free care giving brochure on how to choose a nursing home or assisted living facility.
    www.leadingage.org
    202-783-2242
- The Assisted Living Facility Association of America, www.alfa.org
    Checklist on how to evaluate facilities.
    703-691-8100 ext. 204
- Children of Aging Parents, www.careguide.com
    Free publication list on elder-care topics
- National Association for Home Care, www.nahc.org
    202-547-7424

In addition, see the exhaustive resource guide at the conclusion of this book.

QUESTION
How do I know if I should consider long-term care insurance?

Ask yourself these questions:
- Can I afford to pay the premiums?
- How much coverage do I need?
- Will I qualify for the coverage?
- Do I have children that would desire for me to live with them should I lose my health?

CHAPTER NINE

THE MEDICAID SPEND-DOWN PROCESS: PROTECTING WHAT YOU'VE SPENT A LIFETIME ACCUMULATING

Talk is cheap except when Congress does it.
—Mark Twain

IN THE FEBRUARY 2005 edition of *Consumer Reports Money Adviser*, Americans over age 65 were asked about their greatest fear regarding retirement. Forty-two percent had a fear of running out of money before they die. If you do not have Long-term Health Care Insurance, you are probably concerned as well about protecting your assets from Medicaid Spend-Down if nursing home care should become necessary.

The term Medicaid, especially to seniors, often brings a negative connotation since it is sometimes equated with welfare. Though welfare uses Medicaid dollars, nursing home care is a completely different issue. In 2004, 43% of the $115 billion spent in nursing homes was paid by Medicaid, according to the July, 2006 Kaiser Family Foundation fact sheet.

HISTORY AND CHANGES IN MEDICAID LAW

Prior to September 30, 1989, when a spouse (Sam) entered a nursing home, the remaining spouse (Sue) would be required by Medicaid to pay Sam's expenses until only $3000 remained in their savings. At that point, Sue was left destitute, yet her financial needs continued. So after all the years of saving and sacrifice, Sue was left impoverished. How was she supposed to live? How was she supposed to pay her bills? What if she had no living relatives to help? This is an example of a hard-working, taxpaying individual, who was virtually left penniless. What was she supposed to do?

> *Medicaid is neither welfare nor entitlement.*

Finally, after many spouses like Sue were left destitute, Congress made a major change in Medicaid by approving Public Law # 100-360 Section 4133 on September 30, 1989. The purpose of this law is to provide assistance for the at-home spouse (also known as the community spouse) to avoid a total spend-down of assets. This law would have allowed Sue to live with a sense of financial dignity. This benefit is neither welfare nor entitlement. The money comes from *our* tax dollars set aside for each state.

Medicare and Medicaid were signed into law on July 30, 1965, by then-president Lyndon B. Johnson. Since 1965 there have been many pieces of legislation that have brought about changes culminating in the Deficit Reduction Act of 2005 (DRA) which radically impacted Medicaid laws.

When attempting to qualify for Medicaid, there are two specific areas to consider: income and assets.

Understanding Medicaid

Each state has an income and an asset guideline for qualifications. Check with your state's Medicaid office for current eligibility requirements.

What are the basic Medicaid eligibility requirements?
- Minimum age of 65 or disabled.
- Resident of the state in which you are qualifying.
- Must be a medical necessity.
- Admission into a certified care facility with a minimum stay of 30 days.
- Your monthly income should be no greater than your state dictates. (The limit for Texas in 2015 was $2,911 per month.)
- Total countable assets (see "Asset Options") for applicant must not exceed $2000.
- These numbers are subject to change from year to year.

When attempting to qualify for Medicaid, there are two specific areas to consider: income and assets. I will deal with the solutions to these issues after describing the qualifications.

A. Income Qualifications

Sources: Social Security, earned income (if the at-home spouse still works), passive income from investments, IRA distributions. Some states have their own income limit to qualify for Medicaid, while others do not regulate income. So what can you do if your income exceeds the Medicaid limits for qualification?

1. **Dispose of excess income**

    Social Security and pensions cannot be transferred to the at-home spouse. However, you can dispose of the assets that are generating the excess income which could cause you to exceed the threshold for qualification. These other incomes include, but are not limited to, producing mineral rights and rent payments which *can be* transferred to the at-home spouse.

2. **Purchase a Qualified Income Trust (QIT)**

    If an applicant's income is still over the allowable amount, you must purchase a Qualified Income Trust (QIT), formerly known as a Miller Trust. This trust allows individuals whose income exceeds the Medicaid limits to still qualify. This is accomplished by placing all income above the qualifying income limit each month into the QIT. You can establish this account at your local bank. The

Medicaid division of Health and Human Services is the beneficiary of this account upon the applicant's death. The attorney who drafts your QIT should work closely with the Medicaid case worker assigned to you in order to provide a smooth transition during qualification.

B. Asset Tests

Exempt assets (those assets that are protected) include your homestead with equity up to $500,000 (some states up to $750,000), household and personal goods, one automobile of any value, an Irrevocable Funeral Services Contract and life insurance cash values with death benefits under $1500. The remaining assets can be handled in the following manner:

1. The at-home spouse may have to liquidate the applicant's qualified monies, such as 401(k)s, 403(b)s, IRAs, and Self Employed Pension Plans depending on the total account values.
2. If you are an at-home spouse, you have a Protected Resource Allowance (PRA). This amount is 50% of your combined countable assets, with a $104,400 limit. These countable assets include bank accounts, CDs, money markets, mutual funds, stocks, bonds, deferred annuities, life insurance cash value over $1500, real estate other than homestead and safety deposit box collectables.

What can you do as an at-home spouse whose accounts exceed the Protected Resource Amount (PRA) limit?
1. Spend down the assets until your spouse qualifies.
2. Pay off debts with the excess amount, whether personal or household, and whether in the applicant's or spouse's name.
3. Do repairs and necessary upgrades to the house.

-OR-

4. The PRA can potentially be expanded beyond the normal PRA if the joint income is less than the Medicaid threshold. Refer to the glossary for terminology on the protected resource amount.
5. Purchase a Qualified Pension Annuity. This will convert the asset (which needs to be spent-down) to an income for the at-home spouse. The contract must be set up as an irrevocable, un-assignable, immediate income annuity. In most states this allows you to convert the asset to a qualified income, which protects the at-home spouse from spending down the asset.

Once qualified for Medicaid there are events which could potentially disqualify you.

WARNING:

Once qualified for Medicaid there are events which could potentially disqualify you. For example, the Medicaid recipient must be removed as beneficiary from all legal documents. Ask siblings or anyone else who would have named you, the Medicaid recipient, as their beneficiary to remove your name and place the next person in line for that asset. If they don't do this, it could potentially endanger your status: it would change your status to private pay until the inheritance is fully spent on the recipient's care.

MEDICAID ESTATE RECOVERY PROGRAM (MERP)

In March of 2005, the Department of Aging and Disability Services (DADS) implemented the Medicaid Estate Recovery Program (MERP). This act enables Medicaid to seek recovery of expenses from a Medicaid recipient's estate upon their death. This question has become paramount for many. Why does Medicaid have the ability to file a Class 7 claim to recover expenses in probate court upon the sale of the homestead, and more importantly, is there anything I can do about it?

It is important to note that *MERP only recovers estate property that is subject to and is probated in court.*

Exemptions exist: If a surviving spouse or a single adult child has been living in the home for at least 12 months prior to the recipient's death, then the state does not seek recovery. Typically, no action is taken if recovery is not cost effective. There is no estate recovery if there is a surviving disabled child (any age) living at that time.

What if my House is in a Revocable Living Trust?

If you are applying for Medicaid for your spouse or parent you must remove the home from a Revocable Living Trust. You will then place the homestead back into the at-home spouse's name *only*. If there is no at-home spouse, the house still must be removed from the Trust so that the state can potentially recover their expenses by filing a probate claim on the property at your death.

How to Avoid Medicaid Estate Recovery on Your Homestead

You can potentially convey real estate through an Enhanced Estate Deed, also known as a Special Warranty Deed with reservation of life estate. This deed takes away the necessity of probate which allows you to pass the homestead to your heirs.

If I am moving into a nursing home and applying for Medicaid, can I rent out my home?

If you are vacating your home and moving to a nursing home, you probably should not rent out your home. If the rent pushes you, the applicant, over the income cap for Medicaid qualification, it will affect your eligibility. A better choice would be to allow someone to live in the home and pay the taxes, insurance, and utility bills.

Key Changes as a Result of the 2005 Deficit Reduction Act

Converting countable or available assets to exempt assets (those you get to keep) is not as easy as it used to be, due to the Deficit Reduction Act. Let's review a few of these updated rules:

1. Structured monthly gifts are no longer an effective method of asset preservation.
2. The penalty period now begins when all other requirements of eligibility have been met, rather than when the last asset transfer occurred.
3. The "look-back" period to keep track of asset transfers has been extended for families from three to *five years*.
4. Any payments from a Medicaid-qualified annuity that an at-home spouse has initiated must go to the state to pay Medicaid costs for the ill spouse when the well spouse dies. However, the children can be secondary or contingent beneficiaries should Medicaid make their recovery and there is still money left in the annuity.
5. Home equity in excess of $500,000 or at a state's option $750,000, is now considered a countable asset.
6. The new home-equity cap rule does not apply if a well spouse remains in the home, regardless of its value, but would apply if the well spouse died.
7. Under the "income first" initiative, when setting the well spouse's allowed income, states must consider all income available to the sick spouse, which in practice

may reduce the amount of the protected resource allowance permitted for the healthy or well-spouse.
8. The Long-Term Care Partnership program allows all states to relax asset limits in Medicaid eligibility cases when individuals have taken out long-term care insurance policies that conform to the standards of the National Association of Insurance Commissioners (NAIC).
(Based on The Deficit Reduction Act of 2005, as summarized in: www.eldercareanswers.com, and the Kaiser Family Foundation's website: www.kff.org)

Every state has a Medicaid program that is funded with state and federal money. There are federal guidelines, as well as individual state requirements for qualification.

The Federal Government enacted the Deficit Reduction Act (DRA) in 2005. In February of 2006, most states changed the "look-back" period regarding money moved out of the name of the Medicaid applicant to a non-spouse from three years to five years. Each state has a penalty period regarding the transfer of assets from your personal estate to another individual. Those assets that moved out of your estate prior to February 8, 2006 are subject to pre-DRA rules and those after February 8, 2006 will be subject to post-DRA rules.

Every state has a Medicaid program that is funded with state and federal money.

WHERE CAN I LEARN MORE?

The Financial Aid Center for Long-Term Care is an organization that specifically studies the Medicaid dilemma. Their website is www.MedicaidHelp.com and they have a program called MAPP, Medicaid Asset Protection Plan. If you do not have Long-Term Care Insurance and need to know about your state laws and what your Medicaid options are, you might want to contact this organization. There is a fee; however, knowing what can and cannot be done may be much less costly than not knowing and going to an attorney first.

THE FOUR MEDICAID MYTHS

Myth #1: Once a person is in a nursing home their money can only be spent on their care if they ever hope to qualify for Medicaid.

Fact: There is no requirement in the Medicaid rules that specifies how a patient's money is to be spent. The only limitation is that you need to deal with the invalid transfer or lack of fair market compensation rules when it comes time to apply for Medicaid.

Myth #2: You are not allowed to dispose of assets for the purpose of becoming qualified for Medicaid.

Fact: You are free to spend however you choose, but what you cannot do is dispose of assets for the *purpose* of becoming qualified for Medicaid and then fail to disclose that fact at the time of application. That could be considered Medicaid fraud.

As far as Medicaid is concerned, there is nothing to keep you from disposing of assets for any reason, as long as you abide by the Medicaid rules, including the invalid transfer rules and procedures. As long as you are willing to disclose to Medicaid what you have done, and accept the penalty that they impose—a period of ineligibility—there will be no problem. Ineligibility is in proportion to the value of the transferred asset, not a specific time period. Hence, the more you transfer the longer the period of ineligibility.

Myth #3: If you give away anything, you then have to wait five years before you can qualify for Medicaid.

Fact: The period of disqualification is a function of the value of the gift and the state's private pay factor, not a specific period of time.

Myth #4: Even if you wanted to give gifts, you are somehow limited to a maximum gift per year.

Fact: There is no limit on the value of a gift that can be made from one person to another. Another version of that same myth says that although you may be able to give it away, you or the recipient will pay a substantial gift tax on anything over $12,000 per year. Again, this is false. If the total of the lifetime gifts

There is no need for panic if you find yourself in a situation where you or a loved one needs to quality for medicaid.

by the donor does not exceed one million dollars (under the current Federal Gift and Estate Tax system) then there is no tax to pay.

(Myths/Facts adapted from MAPP supplemental information.)

SUMMARY

There is no need for panic if you find yourself in a situation where you or a loved one needs to qualify for Medicaid. Simply take time to educate yourself, and become familiar with your state Medicaid program. Being prepared always leads to a better outcome; however, if you are unaware of your options, the consequences can be costly.

Don't wait until the last minute to plan. If you do not have Long-Term Care Insurance, knowing your options in advance is the key to protecting what you have spent a lifetime accumulating.

CHAPTER TEN

STRETCH IRAS: HOW TO CREATE WEALTH AND PASS IT TO YOUR HEIRS

Man's mind, stretched to a new idea, never goes back to its original dimension.

–Oliver Wendell Holmes

FINANCIAL PLANNERS TELL YOU to stretch your IRA, but they don't want to show you how. Ever wondered why? It's simple. They want you to transfer your IRA to them first so they can get the commissions, then they will show you how to stretch it. This chapter will show you how to stretch your IRA and to whom you may stretch it without unnecessarily transferring it to a broker.

In April 2002, the Department of Treasury released simplified and improved regulations regarding the distribution of IRAs. The regulations *reduced* the minimum annual distributions that we must make during our retirement years. These changes make it easier to pass qualified money to our heirs. This creates the opportunity for the Stretch IRA.

What Is a Stretch IRA?

A Stretch IRA is a strategy which allows you to continue to tax defer your IRA to your heirs once you are deceased. This potentially allows you to leave a financial legacy for generations.

Since U.S. life expectancy is generally somewhere in the late 70s to late 80s, the unused portion of an IRA that can be rolled to the spouse or stretched for non-spouse beneficiaries. In the past, children would receive the IRA distribution upon the benefactor's death. They would then either take a lump-sum distribution which was immediately taxable, or they could take a five year payout, which would spread the tax liability. Today, if your spouse is your primary beneficiary and your children are your contingent (successor beneficiaries), guess what? You have a Stretch IRA.

The term Stretch IRA was actually created by an organization called the Wealth Advisory Group, in 1999. Others call it a Legacy IRA, or a multigenerational IRA. Whatever you call it, you can see that it is a planning strategy we can utilize under IRS code, section 691, regarding passing assets to our decedents. (See title 26 of the Internal Revenue Code.)

How it Works

Some consider stretching an IRA as a tool to "control your assets beyond the grave." Of course, the assumption is that you will not live to be 103. Therefore, you can pass all or part of your IRA money to your heirs. This allows them to use the IRS *single life expectancy table* based on *their* age, which reduces the required amount of annual distribution. By reducing the mandatory distribution, this allows the money more time to grow and therefore, to compound. For example, a 76

> *No wonder Einstein called compound interest the "Eighth wonder of the World."*

year old passes away and leaves a $100,000 IRA to his son, who is 50 years old. If the son stretches the IRA, and averages an 8% return per year then when he reaches 76 he will have withdrawn over $450,000 from that inherited IRA.

No wonder Einstein called compound interest the "Eighth Wonder of the World." In theory, if you can convince your heirs to join you in this *multigenerational* idea, you could create wealth that would take the place of Social Security, should it either decrease or terminate.

EXAMPLE OF GENERATIONAL INHERITANCE

Suppose Joe is 70.5 years old and older than his spouse, Mary. Since Joe is over 70.5, he's currently required to withdraw minimum annual distributions (RMD or MRD). Joe makes withdrawals for two years and suddenly passes away. His spouse Mary, who is 67, is the primary beneficiary. Mary can roll Joe's IRA into her own IRA and defer withdrawals until she turns 70.5 years old.

If Mary lists the adult children as primary beneficiaries and grandchildren as contingent beneficiaries, the children who inherit Mary's IRA can then utilize the single life expectancy tables

> *By naming primary and contingent beneficiaries you can stretch your IRA potentially for generations. If your heirs do the same then together you can build a legacy.*
>
> ∽

provided by the IRS. Because of their younger ages, the children can draw out far less money per year, thus stretching out the benefits. This allows the money more years to compound.

When the children inherit the money, they do not roll it over into their own IRA as Mary did. Instead, the money is transferred into a new account called a Beneficiary Designated IRA (BDA) or Inherited IRA. The net effect is that the original IRA and its growth is stretched over multiple generations. To accomplish this, you MUST do it through a Trustee-to-Trustee transfer. Do not have a check mailed to you if you are the beneficiary of an IRA. Doing this will disqualify you from being able to stretch that IRA. Also, this will trigger a large tax liability.

Should your IRA last beyond your children and be passed down to your grandchildren then your grandchildren do not get to use the single life expectancy tables. They must inherit their parent's life expectancy, which allows the IRS to finally cash in on the income tax owed.

By naming primary and contingent beneficiaries you can stretch your IRA potentially for generations. If your heirs do the same then together you can build a legacy.

WARNING:

Never name your estate as primary beneficiary of an IRA because an estate has no *life expectancy*, thereby limiting the IRA withdrawal period.

STEPS TO STRETCHING YOUR IRA

1. Make your beneficiary a person, but not an estate. Name your primary and contingent beneficiaries for *all* of your IRAs.
2. Make sure your intentions are clearly defined and documented on your IRA applications, whether done through a financial planner, bank, or insurance company.
3. If there are multiple heirs, designate the percentage in your IRA account that is to go to each one.
4. Discuss the "stretch your IRA concept" with your beneficiaries. Attempt to make this a family decision for the future. If you have a properly drawn Will or Trust, you can designate that your heirs stretch their portion of the inherited IRA.

WHAT ABOUT ROTH IRAS?

Your spouse can receive your Roth IRA and need not take any distributions, as taxes have already been paid. However, on a *non-spousal inherited* Roth IRA, the IRS makes beneficiaries take distributions just as if it were a traditional IRA, using the single life expectancy tables to make the distributions.

Giving your IRA to a Charitable Organization

Many people choose to give part or all of their IRA distributions to charitable institutions. As long as there is no estate tax due, a Charitable Remainder UniTrust (CRUT) can be an effective tool to pass assets to a charity. The Trust would pay a stream of income to the heirs of your choice for a set term (usually not to exceed 20 years) and the *remainder* would then go the designated charity.

> *Remember that a stretch IRA is a tool the IRS gives you which can provide a generational blessing to family members*

Good News

The Pension Protection Act of 2006 was amended so that a non-spouse beneficiary can do direct transfers/rollovers from a company plan. (The company plan *must* allow the rollover to an inherited IRA for the non-spouse beneficiary.)

Summary

The results of stretching your IRA can be phenomenal. Some salesmen advertise returns that are blown way out of proportion in order to get you to transfer your IRA to their company. For your purposes, just remember that a Stretch IRA is a tool that the IRS gives you which can provide a generational blessing to family members. The more future generations recognize the benefits of delayed gratification, the greater the chance they will enjoy their retirement years. Additionally, it will provide them the opportunity to pass down an inheritance to their children, and their children's children.

CHAPTER ELEVEN

WILLS VS. REVOCABLE LIVING TRUSTS: HOW TO PREVENT HEIR-TO-HEIR COMBAT!

It's not that I'm afraid to die; I just don't want to be there when it happens.

–Woody Allen

COUNTY COURTS WERE ESTABLISHED to probate wills, settle estates, and distribute assets of the deceased as early as the Roman Empire, and could be found in 13th century England, and in the New World. The first actual probate court in the United States was established in Massachusetts in 1784.

Hundreds of years after those earliest Roman courts, the value and process of probate is being challenged. Today, many believe probate is "outdated, overrated and ill-fated." In fact, in the 1960s the New York Bar Association brought suit in an attempt to prevent the sale of Norman Dacey's book, *How to Avoid Probate*. Dacey writes, "Almost universally corrupt, [probate] is essentially a form of private taxation levied by the legal profession upon the rest of the population."

"The truth is that millions of Americans are priced out of the legal system," says attorney James Turner, executive director of Help Abolish Legal Tyranny (HALT), a consumer group that works for the reform of legal practices. Some states allow attorneys to charge 5% of the estate value to settle your estate and pass what's left to your heirs.

> *Almost universally corrupt, [probate] is essentially a form of private taxation levied by the legal profession upon the rest of the population.*
>
> -Norman Dacey

Laying the Groundwork for Legal Documents

Let's start with some basic definitions:
- A **Will** is simply a set of instructions regarding the disbursement of your property upon your death. It is *not* a means of avoiding probate. It is a legal way of informing the probate court of your intentions after you are deceased. Your Will is actually a letter to the probate judge expressing your desires and naming the executor or executors who will help carry out your wishes once your debts and taxes have been paid.
- **Probate** is the court-supervised procedure for proving the authenticity and legality of your Last Will and

Testament. The probate process empowers the judge to bring finality to your decisions and disperse your assets to your legal heirs. Once probate is complete it stops disgruntled heirs from challenging your decisions. However, should your Will be challenged *during* the probate process, by any interested party or beneficiary, the distribution is at the sole discretion of the judge. Over one-third of all wills are successfully challenged, according to Henry Abts.

- A **Trust** is also a set of instructions regarding the disbursement of your assets. However, it is usually written to your successor or joint trustee—*not* a judge. With a Trust, you appoint the successor trustee and give him or her authority to act on your behalf in the distribution of your assets at your death. Property held in a Revocable Living Trust does not pass through probate. The Trust also maintains privacy and confidentiality regarding your real estate and all other financial affairs.

Points to consider with a Will:
- Assets move without probate from one spouse to another on all assets held in Joint Tenants with Rights of Survivorship (JTWROS). In many cases probate may not be necessary at the death of the first spouse. I had a client that was charged $22,000 by an attorney to move real estate property out of the deceased husband's name into her name. That's highway robbery. He could have

simply done an affidavit of heirship and avoided most of the expense, but he chose not to.

- You are required *by law* to place a notice of the death in the newspaper. Do you have any potential claimants?
- A Will does not cover conservatorship. A conservatorship is a court order. It is a legal process in which an adult is appointed by the Court to make financial decisions for another person who is determined to be financially incapable of making those decisions. Many jurisdictions use the term "guardianship of the person" to refer to the same legal principle. *This can be very expensive.*
- What if the probate takes months or years? Your beneficiaries may be required to file a separate income tax return for the probate estate. They may have to file and pay income taxes for the estate during the probate period.
- Probate is public information. Many counties now have probate information online. That means that records of any assets—including money—are publicly open, which allows *any* potentially unscrupulous salesman or con artist to harass your heirs.
- Passing assets to a non-spouse will incur probate-related fees such as: accounting fees, filing fees, court costs, and appraisal fees on properties, together with attorney fees.

Points to Consider With a Revocable or Marital Trust:

- Assets must be placed into the Trust, or funded, in order to avoid probate. Funding the Trust is how you re-title your assets and move them from your name as an individual to your name as trustee. *If this is not done, you have wasted money on the cost of the Trust.* Your Trust should include asset transfer paperwork along with a notarized summary of your Trust, which is sent to all banks, brokerage houses and any other financial entity you wish to notify, in order to avoid the probate process. You must also have your deeds (usually provided with your Trust) re-titled on your property to a quitclaim deed properly drawn by an attorney to place that asset into your Revocable Living Trust.
- You are ordinarily the trustor (the person who puts assets into your trust) and the trustee (the person who manages your assets).
- The initial cost to establish a Trust is generally more than the cost to prepare a Will. It varies somewhere between $1000 to $3500.
- No public notice of death is required with a Trust.
- Your assets held in Trust are "shielded" from the probate courts and are therefore not public record, which protects your privacy.
- You should insist that the attorney drawing up your Trust include instructions for the successor/joint trustee upon your death.

Is There a Way to Keep My Personal Affairs Private?

Oliver Wendell Holmes said many years ago, "Put not your trust in money, but put your money in Trust."

Since your Will only becomes active upon your death, there is no way of keeping your affairs private. In fact, many county clerk's information regarding a decedent's assets and to whom they were given is *public record* and can be accessed from the internet. As stated previously, the Revocable Living Trust, in contrast, is a private legal document created by you to hold title or ownership to your assets. Unlike a Will, a Trust is active during your lifetime even through incapacitation. Upon your death it carries out your wishes to the designated beneficiaries, while avoiding probate and keeping your affairs private.

Is it Harmful to Place My Children's Names on My Assets to Avoid Probate?

If you place your children's names as co-owners on your bank or brokerage accounts, they legally own half of those assets. If any of those children are sued (whether by car wreck, divorce, creditors, bankruptcy or even by the IRS) one half of your money is potentially exposed to those creditors.

You might want to consider a signature account for your children so that they can pay your bills should you become incapacitated or ill over a long period of time. Many attorneys would suggest a Durable General Power Of Attorney for financial affairs. This allows your heirs to carry on your financial affairs and at the same time, protect you from their creditor issues. The Durable General Power Of Attorney ceases upon your death at which time all powers pass to the executor (if you have a will) or the co-trustee or successor trustee (if you have a trust).

WHAT OTHER LEGAL DOCUMENTS DO I NEED IN ADDITION TO A WILL OR TRUST?

- **Durable Power Of Attorney For Health Care** – Appoints someone you trust to make health care decisions for you when you cannot make them for yourself.
- **Durable General Power Of Attorney For Financial Affairs** – Allows someone of your choosing to make financial decisions for you if you are no longer capable of doing it for yourself.
- **Guardianship Protection** – A guardian is a person who has the legal authority (and the corresponding duty) to care for the personal and property interests of another person.
- **Directive to Physicians (Living Will)** – A Living Will usually covers specific directives as to the course of treatment to be taken by caregivers, or in some cases forbidding treatment, even food and water. This document will usually cover your desires concerning life-sustaining treatment, terminal conditions, and irreversible conditions.
- **HIPAA Form** – (Health Insurance Portability &

Accountability Act) This is an authorization for disclosure of confidential health care information for those you trust.

Those who think it is permissible to tell white lies soon become color blind.

–Austin O'Malley

Beware of banks and attorneys who want to base the price of your Trust on the size of your estate. In most cases, that is a marketing ploy. The size of your estate rarely has anything to do with the cost of the Trust. AB provisions are necessary for large estates (those over $3.5 million per individual or $7 million per couple in 2009), which should still only incur a nominal charge. If you are simply placing accounts into your trust and re-titling the asset—from your name as an individual to your name as a trustee—why should that cost you more money?

Beware of banks and attorneys who want to base the price of your Trust on the size of your estate.

What Your Attorney May Not Want You to Know

If you have no real estate, your assets are modest and you don't have concerns about your children fighting over your estate, there is something you can do to avoid probate other than purchasing a Revocable Living Trust. With brokerage accounts, you can contact your agent or firm and ask for their Transfer on Death (TOD) forms and place your preferred designations on all of your non-qualified brokerage accounts to avoid the time and expense of probate. You can also avoid probate by designating your bank accounts as Paid on Death (POD).

Both of these designations, TOD and POD, simply name beneficiaries *in advance,* allowing you to pass that money to your heirs probate-free. Your annuities and life insurance policies avoid probate because you should have designated primary and contingent beneficiaries when you purchased them. This is what you are now doing on your brokerage and bank accounts with the TOD and POD forms—naming beneficiaries in order to avoid probate. Attorneys make money based on your lack of knowledge, which is why they don't tell you about the TOD and POD forms.

Another ploy commonly used by attorneys is to sell you a Testamentary Trust, as opposed to a Revocable Living Trust. A Testamentary Trust does not avoid probate; however, most people choose a Trust *in order to* avoid probate. The attorney is playing on your ignorance regarding this distinction because he can now charge you for the Trust and still probate your estate.

Henry W. Abts III, author of *The Living Trust*, is considered by many to be the foremost authority on Living Trusts. He writes, "The Testamentary Trust is the best of both worlds for the attorney, who collects a substantial fee for drawing up the Trust now and a probate fee later."

Another ploy often used by attorneys is to convince you that a Will is all you need. They claim it is "less expensive" than a Revocable Living Trust. They make statements like "your estate is not large enough for a trust." They end their sales pitch with statements like: "...besides, our state is a probate-friendly state." In most cases he is only saying this to get you to purchase a Will, which he makes money on *today*, so that he can probate your estate and make money *tomorrow*.

I have seen attorneys try to scare people, *especially those over age 65*, that don't have properly drawn HIPAA forms. One group of attorneys was trying to get their potential clients to pay $500 for this form. This form is available in most doctor's offices at no cost. So when I say look for a "qualified" attorney, I am not just speaking of his competencies, but also his ethics.

PREVENTING HEIR-TO-HEIR COMBAT

The average time for probate in the U.S. is 18 months. The breakdown for probate costs is around 70% for attorney fees and 30% for court costs. (You can readily see that the real issue may be more about avoiding *attorneys* at death than the actual probate process. Just a thought!)

There are multiple types of Trusts: Special Needs Trusts for disabled heirs, Life Insurance Trusts, Irrevocable Trusts or Miller Trusts. These trusts address issues *other* than avoiding probate and keeping your affairs private.

The main purpose of this chapter is to compare the differences between Wills and Revocable Living Trusts. I want to end this chapter with an illustration of who should consider a Will and who should consider a Trust:

Who Should Consider a Will	Who Should Consider a Trust
• Estate valued from $50,000 to $100,000 • No home or other real estate • Only one beneficiary • Not concerned about probate costs or time	• Estate valued over $100,000 • Own home or other real estate (especially out of state) • Multiple beneficiaries or blended families • Disabled heirs • Lock in costs

Regardless of the document you choose, make sure that you have the additional financial and healthcare powers to finish out your legal document portfolio. Doing so can give you great peace of mind!

FOR THE "DO-IT-YOURSELFER"

Here are a couple of websites that will help you with legal documents should you want to have a more hands-on approach to addressing the cost for legal documents: www.nolo.com and www.legalzoom.com

QUESTION

Are you saying that everyone should have a Revocable Living Trust?

No, but I am saying that knowing your options and reviewing your situation are factors to consider in order to make wise decisions on your personal legal documents.

Do most people need legal advice when putting together their documents?

I believe so. A qualified attorney will be able to walk you through all the documents and potential pitfalls to avoid "heir-to-heir" combat. Plus, if you decide that a Revocable Living Trust is the best document for you and you are over the age of 65, you will need to make sure that your property deed is properly drawn so you do not lose your over-65 exemption on school or property taxes.

CHAPTER TWELVE

INVESTMENT ADVISOR OR BROKER: WHO SHOULD I CHOOSE TO INVEST MY MONEY?

> *Wall Street is the only place that people ride to in a Rolls-Royce to get advice from those who take the subway.*
> —Robert T. Kiyosaki, *Rich Dad, Poor Dad*

FOR DECADES, THE RETAIL brokerage industry has been all that the consumer has known. This side of the securities industry is just as heavily commission-driven as the insurance industry.

I recently saw a commercial for E-Trade. It depicted a fellow in a lavish room trying to pick up his cup of coffee, yet he was shaking so badly he could not bring the cup to his lips. The inference was that he feared his clients would find out about working directly with a discount brokerage firm and he would lose his client base!

Arthur Levitt, former chairman of the Securities & Exchange Commission, states, "Sadly, the brokerage industry still has numerous flaws. That's not to say that all brokers are commission-hungry wolves on the prowl for naïve investors. Some are; others are just inept. Most are honest professionals. They are good people stuck in a *bad system*."[20]

In his book, *Four Pillars of Investing*, William Bernstein writes, "Few industries are as opaque to serious study as retail brokerage. The most basic data pertaining to broker background and performance, portfolio turnover, and expense simply *do not exist*." Vanguard founder John Bogle says of Bernstein's book, "It's the book that I wish I'd written myself."

We can learn from the wisdom of Arthur Levitt, "They want you to buy stock you don't own and sell the ones that you do, because that's how they make money for themselves and their firms. They earn commissions *even* when you lose money."[21]

Scott Burns, author and syndicated columnist, warns: "What does this mean for most of us? It means about 95 percent of all the people who are called 'financial adviser' are working on commission.... By itself this isn't an evil plot. I know some very fine brokers who have built their book of business by guiding investors into low-expense mutual funds, such as the American Funds family. But they are a rarity. Most 'financial advisers' peddle the anointed garbage of the week.... If these

---

[20] Arthur Levitt, *Take On The Street: What Wall St. and Corporate America Don't Want You to Know / What You Can Do to Fight Back*, 2002, Random House, Chapter 1.

[21] Arthur Levitt, *Take On The Street: What Wall St. and Corporate America Don't Want You to Know / What You Can Do to Fight Back*, 2002, Random House, Chapter 1.

folks were doctors, researchers would observe that the cost of their prescriptions is more harmful than doing nothing."[22]

POTENTIAL DISADVANTAGES OF USING A RETAIL BROKER

You cannot watch the evening news without hearing revelations of a new Wall Street scandal involving corrupt practices, such as kickbacks, accepting bribes, misleading advertising and outright theft. What you may not realize is that these scandals come not only from the *commission*-based side of the business, but many hedge funds and big banks themselves have been caught manipulating markets in various ways. Mutual Fund companies and brokerage firms have been caught by the Securities & Exchange Commission with over $3.5 billion pilfered from investors in the last four years alone! The Securities & Exchange Commission (SEC) is currently in the process of returning the $3.5 billion in fines levied; moreover, the SEC is telling Congress that they are going to establish an office that focuses solely on this issue.

According to Ric Edelman, author of *The Lies About Money*, "…investigators from the NASD, SEC, New York Stock Exchange, and several state attorney generals… continue to uncover mischief and wrongdoing in the retail mutual fund world."

If that isn't enough to dissuade you from the retail invest-

---

[22] Scott Burns, "What Financial Adviser Means 95 Percent of the Time," *The Dallas Morning News*, February 29, 2008.

ment world, keep in mind:
- Your retail broker is a salesperson first and foremost.
- He or she may give biased recommendations.
- It is very difficult to identify the actual charges and costs.
- He or she makes money even if you don't.
- He or she has little motivation to manage your money once the commission is paid.

Registered Investment Advisors

Is there an alternative to using a retail broker? Yes. The professional services of fee-only advisors to manage your money can be found through Registered Investment Advisory firms. One of the most important things for you to know is that a Registered Investment Advisor (RIA) and their Investment Advisor Representatives (IAR) have a *fiduciary* responsibility regarding how they invest your assets. The Investment Advisor's fiduciary duty is like that of a lawyer, a CPA, a trustee, or an executor of an estate. In other words, he has a *legal obligation* to put your interests above his own or his firms. For that very reason many retail brokerage firms do not want that additional responsibility as a firm, so they stay strictly on the retail/com-

> *The real problem with the variable annuity is not the concept of tax deferral on the growth of mutual funds, but the complication and layers of confusion built into the products.*

mission side of the securities business.

Liz Pulliam Weston, columnist for MSN Money, asks, "Can You Trust Your Financial Adviser?"

"It's a $10 word, but not knowing it could cost you a fortune. The word is 'fiduciary,' and in the world of money it means someone who's committed to putting your financial interests ahead of his or her own. The word is important because true fiduciaries are harder to find than you might think. Most of the people who want to give you advice about your money aren't held to that high standard. At best, they're held to a 'suitability' standard, which means they're supposed to reasonably believe that the investment and insurance products they want you to buy are appropriate for your situation. Just 'appropriate'–not 'the best choice' or 'in your best interests.'"[23]

Registered Investment Advisors are not immune to conflict, but are less likely to make decisions motivated by greed because their compensation is tied to your financial success. There is a saying in the industry that "compensation determines behavior." This is true as it relates to retail brokers as well as annuity salesmen.

Warning: Using a retail brokerage firm can be hazardous to your financial health!

---

[23] Liz Pulliam Weston, "Can You Trust Your Financial Adviser?" *MSN Money*.

"Picking the right person to look after your money is vital. I'm convinced that knowing the talent you're hiring and knowing what the talent is buying with your money is the paramount consideration in mutual fund investing."

–Louis Rukeyeser, *Mutual Funds Magazine*, January 2005

Registered Investment Advisors and their representatives are independent advisors who charge for their investment advice or charge a management fee. The fee is usually by the hour, or based on a percentage of your assets.

Again, referencing the previously quoted Scott Burns article, of the 232,000 people who call themselves financial advisors, only 13,000 are truly *independent* investment advisors. A word of caution: Many of the nationally recognized retail brokerage firms have begun to operate as fee-based advisors.

Advantages of Independent Investment Advisors

- They offer true no-load funds.
- They may have a greater variety of fund options.
- They function as *fiduciaries* regarding your account.
- They offer unbiased investment advice.
- You know exactly what you are being charged.
- They are typically able to buy funds at a lower cost.
- They can purchase Exchange Traded Funds (ETFs) which are generally cheaper than index mutual funds.

Exchange traded funds can be more tax efficient when it comes to capital gains distributions. ETFs can be sold at "real time" versus mutual funds, which are sold at closing day value. A traditional broker can also purchase these investments for a one-time fixed cost.

An army of principle can penetrate where an army of solders cannot.

–Thomas Paine

Most seniors, and the general public for that matter, do not realize they can access a fee-only advisor, and purchase no-load, no commission, no surrender charge investments. However, this option became available in 1984 when Charles Schwab introduced 140 no-load funds to the general public. Then in 1992, they introduced a no-transaction fee group of mutual funds called One-Source™, making mutual funds easier, less expensive, and accessible to the American consumer. No-commission, fee-based investing is becoming one of America's wisest investment choices. Fidelity, Charles Schwab, TD Ameritrade, Vanguard and others provide this option.

> **The insurance industry's commission-based variable annuities tend to be nothing more than fear-driven products.**

Forecasting can be difficult, especially when it concerns the future.

–Robert T. Kiyosaki

INVESTMENT OPTIONS

1. **Invest It Yourself**
   There are many websites, financial newsletters, magazines, and discount brokerage houses offering mutual funds, index funds, or exchange-traded funds. Check with E-Trade, E-signal, ScottTrade or the Money Paper Guide (www.DirectInvesting.com).

2. **Get Help** – You have two choices:
   a. Hire a retail broker who charges a commission to manage your portfolio. Retail brokers typically do *not* hold a series 65 or 66 securities license unless they are with a dually-licensed firm. They are not fiduciaries unless they hold one of these licenses.
   b. Retain the services of an Independent Investment Advisor, who is a fiduciary and legally required to put your interests before his.

3. **Hire an Investment Advisor Representative**
   This type of advisor is a fiduciary who holds a Series 65 Securities License and must make decisions in your best interest. There are no hidden fees. The advisor fee

is clearly identified on the statement. The charge is a percentage of your portfolio or by the hour. The fees are also potentially deductible on your tax return for your qualified or non-qualified money. Commissions are part of the basis of the stock or fund and are therefore also able to be written off, indirectly.

INVESTMENT SUMMARY

Arthur Levitt Jr. on how to fire your broker:
"If you have less than $50,000 to invest, you don't need a broker. The strategy that makes the most sense is investing in low-cost mutual funds, especially index funds that match performance of a stock index....
If you have more than $50,000 to invest, you should *fire* your broker and find an investment advisor. Brokerage firms would like you to think that they perform the same function as investment advisors.... But they are not the same as independent investment advisors."[24]

Whatever your choice, become a student of the costs when allowing someone else to manage your money. Remember, it is going to take some effort on your part to protect and preserve what you've spent a lifetime accumulating.

---

[24] Arthur Levitt, *Take On The Street: What Wall St. and Corporate America Don't Want You to Know / What You Can Do to Fight Back*, 2002, Random House, Chapter 1.

QUESTION
Are you saying there are no honest, trustworthy brokers?

No, I agree with Arthur Levitt, when he stated that some retail brokers are good people caught in a bad system.

CHAPTER THIRTEEN

Armed and Dangerous: The "Ten Safeguards"

> *They must find it difficult...Those who have taken authority as the truth, rather than truth as the authority.*
>
> —Gerald Massey

IT SHOULD BE CLEAR to you by now that there truly is a *war* being waged for your money. *Disinformation* is most harmful when it is mixed with a seed of truth, making it impossible for you to make accurate decisions.

Some companies make it their number-one goal to hire agents who can help them tap into the senior market. They know that seniors control the majority of the nation's wealth. That is why it is *imperative* for you to be able to recognize who has a legal *and* fiduciary responsibility when it comes to investing your money.

In writing this book, I wanted to be fair to the industries I examine; furthermore, I also wanted to be as factual as possible so you can clearly identify your options.

> *You are looking for someone who is knowledgeable as well as trustworthy.*
>
> ∽

Being equipped with accurate information, however, does not make your job easy. You need to find an Investment Advisor, because he or she are the only ones who have a fiduciary responsibility to do what's in your best interest. You will still have to interview Investment Advisors in order to find one who charges a modest fee (1-1.5%) and has the experience you need. This places you at a vantage point where it will be difficult for anyone to manipulate you.

There are creative designations, bogus designations, insurance-only designations and, most importantly, the true designations for an Investment Advisor. This chapter will empower you with the information you need to answer the question posed in chapter one, "Will the real Investment Advisor please stand up?"

Even if your financial planner holds the highest level of education available (Certified Financial Planner or Series 7 Licensing) there is no guarantee that he will put your needs ahead of his own. You are looking for someone who is knowledgeable as well as trustworthy.

> *Everyone is entitled to their own opinion, not their own facts.*
>
> –Patrick Daniel Moynahan

Patience is a Virtue

If you are to maintain the lifestyle you've grown accustomed to, you must set some reasonable goals, find a trustworthy advisor, and be patient. John Bogle, founder of The Vanguard Group, warns, "Impulse is your enemy." Impatience is a subtle enemy, because it impedes the process necessary to preserve and grow your assets. The Pogo cartoon by Walt Kelly aptly illustrates, "We have met the enemy and he is us."

> ***Impulse is your enemy.***
> -John Bogle, Founder of The Vanguard Group

Be willing to admit when you've made mistakes with your money. Recovery begins with humility. There is an old saying, "Humility is the mother of all virtues." Now is not the time to be proud. Now is the time to be transparent with someone you can trust, someone who can help you get your portfolio back into shape.

> *When you find yourself in a hole, the best thing you can do is stop digging.*
>
> –Warren Buffett

It is up to you to be armed with the right questions and accurate information. These Ten Safeguards are *guaranteed* to smoke out the predators and expose deception. *Ignore them at your own financial risk!*

THE TEN SAFEGUARDS

1. Ask the planner, "How are you compensated?"
   Potential answers:
   - "The company pays me to get your business."
   - "Not one dime of your money is taken to pay me."
   - "One hundred percent of your money goes to work for you on day one."

   Insight:
   All the above answers clearly identify this planner as an insurance agent selling commission-based annuities, which may carry long-term surrender charges.

2. If the planner is trying to sell you an annuity, ask "What particular education do you have that assures that you can effectively follow the market indexes each year to grow my assets?"

   Insight:
   If he stumbles and stammers at this point, show him the door. Remember, an insurance agent rarely knows anything about stock market index options.

3. Ask him, "What are you specifically licensed to sell?"

   Insight:
   If he is a securities licensed agent, *but is primarily pushing indexed annuities,* you now know he is chasing commissions rather than practicing estate planning. Walk away!

4. Ask the planner, "How long have you been licensed in the business?"
   Insight:
   If he says less than 10 years, be wary. Why? He hasn't seen and responded to enough significant market changes. You cannot afford a novice at this stage in your investment life.

5. Ask the planner, "Are you a captive agent?"
   Insight:
   This lets you know that your product choices are limited to what that *one* company offers. If the agent claims to represent several companies, get the names of the companies represented so that you may investigate their ratings and solvency. Being a captive agent, his products are limited; however, being an independent agent does not automatically guarantee that he will sell you the best product. He may sell you the product that pays him the highest commission.

   > **Remember: It is up to you to be armed with the right questions and accurate information!**

6. Ask the planner, "What financial designations do you hold?" Then ask, "Does that designation comes under the jurisdiction of the Securities & Exchange Commis-

sion (SEC) or FINRA (Financial Industry Regulatory Authority)?"

Insight:

Study the graph provided later in this chapter to see if the planner is hiding behind a creative designation!

7. If you are confident in the fact that the planner is securities licensed then ask, "Do you represent a retail brokerage or a fee-based firm?"

Insight:

This will let you know if he is commission-driven (retail brokerage) or fee-based (Investment Advisor). Remember, fees can potentially be deducted as an expense on your tax return on qualified and non-qualified investments, but commissions cannot.

8. Ask the planner, "Does your licensing hold you to a *fiduciary* responsibility (Series 65) regarding my assets?" Then ask, "Is your firm a Registered Investment Advisory firm and are you an investment advisor representative?"

Insight:

This is the type of planner most people need. If he is also a Certified Financial Planner (CFP), all the better for you, if you believe him to be trustworthy. Go to the Securities & Exchange website to confirm his designation: www.AdviserInfo.sec.gov/IAPD

9. Ask the planner, "Have you ever had a written complaint?"

   Insight:
   If he says "yes," confirm his statement with his broker dealer or with your State Board of Insurance, the SEC, FINRA, or state securities regulators.

10. Ask the planner, "Will you be working with me directly or will another member of your organization will be my primary contact?" If someone else then ask, "How long has that person been licensed in the business?"

    Insight:
    Many financial planners will move your account over to a less-experienced planner if your account is less than $250,000. Sometimes they will even let the other agent sign your application, which makes the less-experienced agent your "official" agent of record without your knowledge.

A wise man has great power, and a man of knowledge increases strength.

–Proverbs 24:5

ABCs or CFPs?

The Alphabet Soup of Professional and Not-So-Professional Designations

Designation	Insurance License	Securities License	Fiduciary
General agent	Yes	No	No
Representative	Yes	No	No
Certified Estate Planner (CEP)	Yes	Probably Not	No
Certified Senior Advisor (CSA)	Yes	Probably Not	No
Certified Elder Planning Specialist (CEPS)	Yes	Probably Not	No
Certified Retirement Adviser	Yes	No	No
Life Underwriting Training Council (LUTCF)	Yes	Maybe	No
Registered Financial Consultant (RFC)	Yes	Maybe	No
Chartered Investment Counselor (CIC)	Yes	No	No
Certified Senior Specialist (CSS)	Yes	No	No
Million Dollar Round Table (MDRT)	Yes	Maybe	No
Certified Financial Planner (CFP)	Yes	Maybe	Maybe
Chartered Financial Consultant (ChFC)	Yes	Maybe	Maybe
Chartered Financial Analyst (CFA)	Maybe	Yes	Maybe
Attorney	Maybe	Maybe	Yes
Certified Public Accountant (CPA)	Maybe	Maybe	Yes
Investment Advisor Representative (IAR)	Yes	Yes	Yes

The designations that say "no" under Securities License and "no" under Fiduciary make it clear that the designation typically represents a certification issued by insurance industry programs. These people can *only* sell you their annuities or life insurance when it comes to your investment dollars.

> **Education is not the filling of a pail, but the lighting of a fire!**
> -William Butler Yeats

Their slick PowerPoint presentations are typically nothing but a smoke screen to hide their ulterior motives and their lack of true education—period. Keep in mind the phrase "integrity fraud."

> *If you think education is expensive, try ignorance.*
> –Derek Curtis Bok

When looking to improve your portfolio and expand your knowledge, refuse to be rushed by any salesperson. Always decide to decide later. Do your homework and remember this is *your* portfolio, these are the dollars *you* have spent a lifetime accumulating, and a good investment will be available tomorrow, next week, and probably next month.

I have covered legal, medical, and financial issues and options. My hope is that you will review your personal situation and make the choices that create the greatest financial freedom for you and your loved ones. You can make wise decisions when you have the facts at hand and are aware of all your options. Keep in mind these words of Sir Winston Churchill:

"Never give in; never give in, *never, never, never, never*—in anything, great or small, large or petty—never give in, except to convictions of honor and *good sense.*"

Glossary

Many thanks to the American Institute for Economic Research for much of the information in this glossary. See www.aier.org for more.

Active Management: An investment strategy that tries to beat the returns of the financial markets.

Activities for Daily Living (ADL): The ability to dress, bathe, and feed ourselves, as well as continence, and toileting.

Adjustable Rate Mortgage (ARM): a type of mortgage—initiated during the double-digit interest rate period of the 1980s—that primarily protects lenders against large interest rate changes. A single lender may offer several variations. ARMS include provisions for a periodic adjustment of the interest rate and monthly payments. It is based on the one-year Treasury bill interest rate or other rate. The borrower is assuming some risk with an ARM compared with a fixed rate mortgage.

Annuity: A savings contract purchased from a life insurance company. Often it pays the annuitant fixed payments periodically until death in return for an initial lump-sum payment or series of regular premium payments.

Asset Allocation: The process of deciding how your investment dollars will be split among various classes of financial assets, such as stocks, bonds, and cash investments.

Bond: A certificate of contractual debt; a contract between the issuer (debtor) and the holders (creditors) that promises to pay for the use of the funds through interest payments—often a fixed amount paid semi-annually until the bond reaches maturity—and repayment of the principal or par amount of the bond at a specified future date, called the maturity date. A bond does not represent ownership in a firm like a stock does.

Brokerage: The functions performed by a broker. In its narrowest sense this involves locating and combining buyers and sellers of the asset or commodity being brokered.

Certificate of Deposit: Official financial-institution receipt for funds deposited, sometimes called time certificates of deposit. The deposit is for a specific time period at a specified rate of interest. Interest penalties may be charged for early withdrawal. Rates and conditions often vary widely from bank to bank. They may be negotiable or non-negotiable. Maturity terms may extend from over night to many years.

Charitable-Remainder Trust Annuity: A plan gibing the annuitant an income for the remainder of his life, or a beneficiary's life, created by funds or assets transferred to a qualified charity. The plan pays the annuitant a fixed-dollar amount annually for life based on the value of the transferred asset.

Charitable-Remainder Unitrust: A plan giving the annuitant an income for the remainder of his life, or a beneficiary's life, created by transferring assets to a trust administered by a qualified charity or tax-exempt institution that pays the annuitant a fixed percentage of the trust principal value for life.

Churning: An illegal practice wherein a broker, account executive, or account manager may encourage an investor or account to engage in excessive or unnecessary buy and sell (trading) transactions. This is done with the purpose of earning additional commissions or fees or to manipulate prices by creating the appearance of active trading in a given stock.

Codicil: An amendment to a Will. It is a separate document.

Common (or Equity) Stock: A claim on ownership in a firm and to a portion of its profits in the form of dividends. Because of the right to share in the profits of a firm, as a company grows common stockholders receive greater returns through increased dividends, and increases in the market price of the stock.

Corporate Bond: A bond issued by a corporation, in contrast to those issued by states, municipalities, or the U.S. Treasury.

Debit Card: A plastic card that may look and be used like a credit card. Instead of providing the cardholder access to a line of credit, it provides the vendor with immediate access to the cardholder's assets backing the card. A vendor using a point of sale (POS) terminal has the ability to transfer assets on deposit in the cardholder's checking or savings account directly to the vendor's account.

Dow Jones Industrial Average (DJIA): The best-publicized and most frequently quoted stock market indicator. The DJIA measures stock-price movements of 30 large U.S. corporations.

ETF: Funds that are traded like stocks: Unlike mutual funds, EFTs can be traded anytime during each trading day. No capital gains are taxed until the EFT is sold.

Equities: Securities, namely stocks that represent a claim of ownership in a firm and to a share of its profits in the form of dividends.

FDIC Insurance: An acronym for the bank-deposit insurance coverage provided by the Federal Deposit Insurance Corporation. This insurance was established by the Banking Act of 1933 in an attempt to restore public confidence in the banking system during the depression.

Federal Reserves System (FRS): The U.S. central bank, referred to in the financial-services industry and the media as the Fed. Established in 1913, the system consists of 12 independent reserve banks, each serving a geographic reserve region. Each of the 12 regional banks is in turn owned by members in each region. Members are commercial banks and trust companies, which own the regional bank by holding stock in it.

Fiduciary: An individual or organization that performs a specific task (managing assets, executing a will) under legal contract for a beneficiary.

Financial Industry Regulatory Authority (FINRA), - FINRA is responsible for regulatory oversight of all securities firms that do business with the public; professional training, testing and licensing of registered persons; arbitration and mediation; market regulation by contract for The NASDAQ Stock Market, Inc., the American Stock Exchange LLC, and the International Securities Exchange, LLC; and industry utilities, such as Trade Reporting Facilities and other over-the-counter operations. (Wikipedia)

Front End Load: A sales commission (load), the investor pays when buying shares of a mutual fund. No load funds are also an option for the investor.

Full-Service Bank: A commercial bank providing a full range of financial services including: Stocks, bonds, mutual funds, annuities, checking and savings accounts; CDs—both negotiable and nonnegotiable; Eurodollar deposits; commercial paper; trust services; safekeeping facilities; credit life insurance (which repays loans if the borrower dies); limited underwriting and brokerage services; consumer financing and equipment leasing.

Gross Domestic Product (GDP): The market value of the goods and services produced in a country in a given period, usually a year. Using the U.S. as an example, this includes production by foreign companies in the U.S. (such as a Honda auto factory in Ohio) but not overseas production by U.S. companies.

Gross National Product (GNP): The value of the goods and services produced in a given period by companies owned by the citizens of a particular country. With the U.S. as an example, this includes all overseas production by American companies but not production in the U.S. by foreign firms.

Individual Retirement Account (IRA): A tax-deferred investment plan into which an individual wage earner and spouse may deposit a portion of earned income. The earnings of the IRA are not subject to Federal and state income taxation until they are withdrawn.

Inflation Rate: The percentage change in the general level prices measured over a period of time, usually a month or year. The *Consumer Price Index (CPI)* is one of the most frequently used measures of price inflation.

In The Money: The description of a *call option* whose exercise price is below the market price of the underlying security. Or, a *put option* whose exercise price is above the market price of the underlying security.

Index Funds: Mutual funds that will track the movement of a specific market index like the S&P 500.

Individual Retirement Account (IRA): a tax-advantaged way to save for retirement. Investment earnings within a traditional IRA are not taxed until withdrawn from the account.

Investment Adviser: An individual or organization that manages a mutual fund portfolio and makes day-to-day decisions regarding what securities to buy or sell, also called a fund manager.

Load: In reference to mutual funds, a "front-end" load is a fee, or sales commission, when an investor purchases shares; some funds may also assess "tail-end" loads, which are sales fees charged to shareholders who sell out of a fund.

Load Fund: A mutual fund that charges a sales commission, or load. These commissions can be as high as 8.5% of the amount you invest. Why would you invest in a load fund? Good question!

Management Fee: The fee paid by a mutual fund to its investment adviser.

Medicaid Spend down: A voluntary process of "self impoverishment." This is a process in which you (or your loved ones) limit your assets and transition you from private to public resources to cover your nursing home expenses.

Money Market: The market in which short-term debt securities such as negotiable certificates of deposit, commercial paper, and short-term Federal and state debt (bills and notes) are bought and sold.

Money Market Fund (also called a money market *mutual fund*): Fund that specialized in holding short-term securities such as negotiable certificates of deposit of major commercial banks, high-grade commercial paper and commercial notes and obligations, and short-term Federal or state government debt.

Money Market Securities: Short-term debt securities such as negotiable certificates of deposit (CDs) commercial paper and Treasury bills.

Municipal Bond: A contractual debt obligation issued as a long-term bond by state and local governments. These bonds finance public capital projects such as airports, schools, universities, flood-control projects, and many others.

Mutual Fund: An investment company that sells equity (ownership) shares to investors and utilizes the proceeds to purchase stocks, bonds, and/or money market securities.

NASDAQ: The acronym that identifies the National Association of Security Dealers (NASD). This is an electronic recording and quotation system that lists prices for securities traded in the national *over-the counter* (OTC) market.

Net Asset Value (NAV): A measure of value used in the mutual fund market to determine and report a buying and selling price. It is computed by dividing the total value of the fund's investments by the number of shares outstanding.

No-Load: In reference to a mutual fund; a no-load fund charges no fee, or load, when an investor purchases or sells shares.

Out of the Money: The description of a call option whose strike or exercise price is above the market price of the underlying security; or, a put option whose exercise price is below the market price of the underlying security.

Prime Rate (Interest): Historically, that interest rate at which major financial institutions will lend to their principal and most creditworthy customers.

Prospectus: A printed pamphlet or brochure providing information about a firm and its new security issue or a continuing mutual fund issue.

Protected Resource Amount (PRA): A certain amount of the couple's combined assets that the at-home spouse is entitled to keep.

Real Rate of Return: The rate of return adjusted for price inflation.

Respite Care: Unpaid assistance from a friend or family member may require assistance, so they can re-coop.

SEC (Securities and Exchange Commission): An independent body of the Federal Government charged with regulating, investigating, and to a degree, adjudicating transactions in securities markets.

Security: In investments, generally one of the following:
1. A claim on ownership in a firm, represented by stock.
2. A claim on the debt of a firm or government body represented by, for example, a bond, a Treasury note, or commercial paper.
3. Derivative securities, such as options and futures, which derive their values from the securities upon which they are based.

Standard & Poor's 500 Composite Index (S&P 500): A stock index of 400 industrial company stocks, 40 utility, 40 financial and 20 transportation stocks. A measure, like Dow Jones Industrial Average (DJIA), of how the stock markets are performing.

Stock: A claim on ownership in a firm and to a portion of its profits.

Stock Split: A process in which a corporation or mutual fund issues additional stock to stockholders of record at a specified ratio. The number of stock shares grows, but the total value of the company's stock does not. A split may be two for one, three for one, three for two, five for one, and any ration determined by the board of directors. The price is immediately reduced in proportion to the announced split.

Treasury Bill (T-Bill): Short-term—3 months to 1 year—debt instrument of the Federal Government. It does not bear interest, but is sold at a discount. The gain realized is the difference between the discounted purchase price and the face value of $10,000 purchased at its initial sale for $9,600 would have a return of $400. The $400 gain is realized when the T-bill matures after 6 months and its face value of $10,000. T-bills are backed by the faith and credit of the US Treasury.

Treasury Securities: U.S. Treasury bills, notes, bonds, and other Treasury obligations offered in financial markets. These instruments are sold to financial intermediaries (such as brokerage houses and commercial banks), institutional investors (pension funds, mutual funds, insurance companies), and the general public as a means of raising funds to cover the difference between revenues and the cost of running the government, and the cost of redeeming previously issues debt instruments.

Trust: A legal relationship in which assets are managed by one party (the trustee), which takes legal title to the assets, for the benefit of another party.

Unified Tax Credit: An automatic tax exemption that every American receives, where no estate taxes are due.

Variable Annuity: A tax-deferred investment that is much like a mutual fund, but with an insurance "wrapper." Investors in variable annuities typically are guaranteed that they'll receive at least the amount they invested, thanks to a contract that insures their initial investment. Money you make on variable annuities is not taxed until you take it out.

Resources

Aging Services

American Association of Homes and Services for the Aging
2519 Connecticut Ave., NW
Washington, D.C. 20008
202-783-2242 • Fax: 202-783-2255
www.aahsa.org
The website provides information about services and facilities and how to deal with the emotional stresses of care giving, how to plan for long-term care costs, and how to get involved in aging services. Offers a series of free "Consumer Tips" for finding home and community based services, assisted living facilities, nursing homes, and continuing care retirement communities.

Children of Aging Parents
P.O. Box 167
Richboro, PA 18954
1-800-227-7294
www.caps4caregivers.org
Assist caregivers of the elderly with reliable information, referrals and support to ensure quality care of the nation's growing elderly population.

Eldercare Locator
1-800-677-1116

www.eldercare.gov
Service of the U.S. Administration on Aging to help older Americans and their caregivers connect with state and local agencies and community based organizations that help with a variety of issues.

Institute for Aging
1-415-750-4111
http://www.gioa.org
Institute on Aging (IOA) is a community-based, not-for-profit organization that touches the lives of thousands of seniors.

Little Brother – Friends of the Elderly
28 E Jackson Blvd #405
Chicago, IL 60604
312-786-1032 • Fax: 312-786-1067
www.littlebrothers.org
National, non-profit, volunteer-based organization committed to relieving isolation and loneliness among the elderly. Numerous locations across the U.S.

Meals on Wheels Association of America
203 S Union Street
Alexandria, Virginia 22314
703-548-5558 • Fax: 703-548-8024
www.mowaa.org
Provides congregate and home-delivered meals services to people in need.

National Association of Area Agencies on Aging
1730 Rhode Island Ave NW Suite 1200
Washington, DC 20036
202-872-0888 • Fax: 202-872-0057
www.n4a.org
Provides services which make it possible for older individuals to remain in their home, thereby preserving their independence and dignity.

National Association for Continence
P.O. Box 1019, Charleston
SC 29402-1019
1-800-252-3337 • 843-377-0905
www.nafc.org
Supports the public about the causes, prevention, diagnosis, treatments, and management solutions for incontinence.

National Center on Elder Abuse
c/o Center for Community Research and Services
University of Delaware
297 Graham Hall, Newark, DE 19716
302-831-3525 • Fax: 302-831-4225
www.ncea.aoa.gov
Provides elder abuse information to the public and a national elder abuse hotline referral source at 800-677-1116. The website contains many resources and publications.

National Council on the Aging
1901 L Street, NW, 4th Floor, Washington, DC 20036
202-479-1200 • TTY: 202-479-6674
www.ncoa.org
National network which promotes the dignity, self-determination, health and well being of older persons. Regional offices provide training and employment opportunities to low income Americans over age 55.

National Senior Games Association
P.O. Box 82059, Baton Rouge, LA 70884-2059
225-766-6800 • Fax: 225-766-9115
www.nsga.com
Motivates seniors to lead a healthy lifestyle through the senior games movement.

Senior Drivers
AAA Foundation for Traffic Safety

607 14th Street NW Suite 201, Washington, DC 20005
202-638-5944 • Fax: 202-638-5943
www.seniordrivers.org
Demonstrates exercises that can keep an aging body flexible and offers a set of "refresher" tips to help seniors overcome some situations found in everyday driving.

SeniorHealth
National Institutes of Health
www.nihseniorhealth.gov
Online only resource provides a wide range of information on many health topics including Alzheimer's disease, arthritis, balance problems, cancer, diabetes, exercise, hearing loss, medications, and many more.

Education

SeniorNet
900 Lafayette Street #604
Santa Clara, CA 95050
408-615-0699 • Fax: 408-615-0928
www.seniornet.org
Provides older adults education for and access to computer technologies to enhance their lives and enable them to share their knowledge and wisdom.

Employment

Employment Network for Retired Government Experts
www.enrge.us
Online only resource focused on Government employees who want to work in private companies seeking to fill contract jobs in many different industries. The website posts employee resumes only. It does not have

job lists from companies.

Seniors4Hire.org
7071 Warner Avenue #F-466
Huntington Beach, CA 92647
717-848-0996
www.seniors4hire.org
Offers jobs in industries such as financial services, retail, telecommunications and healthcare with companies including Bank of America, Radio Shack, Regal Entertainment, Petco and Countrywide Financial. Job seekers must contact employers directly. Online applications are not available.

Senior Service America
8403 Colesville Road, Suite 1200
Silver Spring, MD 20910-3314
301-578-8900
www.seniorserviceamerica.org
Provides volunteer and employment opportunities for adults over the age of 55 who wish to re-enter the workforce.

FINANCIAL

Consumer Federation of America
1620 I Street NW Suite 200, Washington, DC 20006
202-387-6121
www.consumerfed.org
A service organization which educates the public on consumer issues and offers several publications on financial, insurance and credit topics.

Department of Labor
Frances Perkins Bldg., 200 Constitution Avenue, NW
Washington, DC 20210

866-444-3272
www.dol.gov
Information on your pension rights and how to protect your pension.

Financial Literacy and Education Commission
www.mymoney.gov
Online only resource of the Federal government with information about managing your money and basic financial education.

Insurance Information Institute
110 William Street 24th Floor, New York, NY 10038
800-331-9146
www.iii.org
Helpline resource for consumers with automobile, homeowners and life insurance questions.

Internal Revenue Service
800-829-1040 • TTY: 800-829-4059
www.irs.gov
Information resource on general tax related issues, including tax filings and refunds.

National Association of Insurance Commissioners
444 North Capitol Street NW #701, Washington, DC 20001
202-624-7790
Insurance regulators focus on consumer protection and produce a number of consumer guides.

National Association of Security Dealers/ FINRA
1735 K Street NW, Washington, DC 20006-1506
301-590-6500
www.finra.org
Provides information on investments, savings plans, retirement accounts, mutual funds, stocks, options and futures. Also has data on individual brokers, security firms and investment advisory firms. Handles complaints against broker-dealers for security violations. Has a forum for

the resolution of monetary and business disputes between investors and securities firms.

North American Securities Administrators Association
750 1st Street NE #1140, Washington, DC 20002
202-737-0900
www.nasaa.org
Organization of state securities agencies devoted to investor protection and investor education.

Savings Bonds
Department of the Treasury
Bureau of the Public Debt
P.O. Box 426
Parkersburg, WV 26106-0426
800-722-2678
www.savingsbonds.gov
Website features pages on buying savings bonds online.

Securities and Exchange Commission
Office of Investor Education and Assistance
100 F Street NE, Washington, DC 20549
800-732-0330
www.sec.gov
Helps with investing and consumer protection questions. Protects investors with fair and orderly securities market regulation.

FUNERALS

National Funeral Directors Association
13625 Bishop's Drive, Brookfield, WI 53005-6607
800-228-6332
www.nfda.org

Offers consumer resources on topics such as planning funerals and dispute resolution for complaints regarding funeral homes.

GENERAL SERVICES

Federal Citizen Information Center
P.O. Box 100, Pueblo, CO 81002
888-878-3256
www.pueblo.gsa.gov
Source for answers to questions about federal government programs and services regarding travel, federal jobs, Social Security, Medicare, taxes and Veteran's affairs.

Federal Trade Commission
CRC-240, Washington, DC 20580
877-382-4357
www.ftc.gov
Enforces truthful advertising in business and prevents unfair methods of competition. Offers an affidavit you can use to report an identity theft. Provides consumer rights and credit report information.

Firstgov
1800 F Street NW, Washington DC, 20405
800-333-4636
www.firstgov.gov
Resource for all U.S. Federal Government information including passports, healthcare, federal jobs, Social Security, Medicare and taxes.

Meals on Wheels Association of America
203 S Union Street, Alexandria, Virginia 22314
703-548-5558 • Fax: 703-548-8024
www.mowaa.org
Provides home-delivered meals services to people in need.

HEALTHCARE

1stDentures.com
2200 Mar East Street, Tiburon, CA 94920-1924
www.1stdentures.com
Finds denture dentists in your area with information about affordable dentures, false teeth, prosthodontics and prosthodontists.

All About Vision
800-222-3937
www.allaboutvision.com
If you are 65 and older, have not seen an ophthalmologist in the last three years or more, and do not belong to an HMO or have Veteran's care, call for the name of a volunteer ophthalmologist in your area.

Alzheimer's Association
225 N Michigan Avenue #1700, Chicago, IL 60601-7633
800-272-3900 • TTY : 866-403-3073
http://www.alz.org
A national network of chapters committed to finding a cure for Alzheimer's and helping those affected by the disease.

Alzheimer's Disease Education and Referral Center
MSC 2292
Building 31 Room 5C27
31 Center Drive, Bethesda, MD 20892
800-438-4380 • TTY: 800-222-4225
www.alzheimers.org
Provides comprehensive Alzheimer's disease information from the National Institutes of Health under the U.S. Department of Health and Human Services.

American Association for Geriatric Psychiatry
7910 Woodmont Ave, Suite 1050
Bethesda, MD 20814-3004
301-654-7850 • Fax: 301-654-4137
www.aagpgpa.org
Promotes the mental health and well being of older people and improving the care of those with late-life mental disorders.

American Cancer Society
1599 Clifton Road NE, Atlanta, GA 30329
800-227-2345 • TTY: 866-228-4327
www.cancer.org
Offers programs to prevent cancer and diminish suffering from cancer through education.

American Diabetes Association
1701 North Beauregard Street, Alexandria, VA 22311
800-342-2383
www.diabetes.org
Provides diabetes information to prevent and cure diabetes and to improve the lives of all people affected by diabetes.

American Health Assistance Foundation
22512 Gateway Center Drive, Clarksburg, Maryland 20871
800-437-2423 • Fax: 301-258-9454
www.ahaf.org
Educates the public about age-related and degenerative diseases, including Alzheimer's disease, muscular degeneration, glaucoma and heart disease.

American Heart Association
7272 Greenville Avenue, Dallas, TX 75231
800-242-8721
www.americanheart.org
Provides heart disease and stroke information for effective prevention

and treatment.

American Parkinson Disease Association
135 Parkinson Avenue, Staten Island, NY 10305
800-223-2732 • Fax: 718-981-4399
www.apdaparkinson.org
Provides research, patient and family support and education on Parkinson's Disease.

Arthritis Foundation
P.O. Box 7669, Atlanta, GA 30357-0669
www.arthritis.org
Supports arthritis and related conditions with advocacy, programs, services and research.

Centers for Disease Control and Prevention
Department of Health and Human Services
1600 Clifton Road, Atlanta, GA 30333
800-311-3435
www.cdc.gov
Leads the public health effort to prevent and control infections and chronic diseases of all kinds.

Centers for Medicare and Medicaid Services
All departments- one number
1-800-236-6500
http://www.cms.hhs.gov/

Department of Health and Human Services
200 Independence Avenue SW, Washington, DC 20201
877-696-6775
www.hhs.gov
Provides assistance to people with healthcare needs.

Doc Board
www.docboard.org
Website that checks whether there have been any complaints or disciplinary actions taken against a doctor.

Lighthouse International
Sol & Lillian Goldman Bldg., 111 E 59th Street
New York, NY 10022-1202
800-829-0500 • Fax: 212-821-9707 • TTY: 212-821-9713
www.lighthouse.org
Enables people to overcome vision impairment through vision rehabilitation services, education, research and advocacy.

Medical Information Bureau
P.O. Box 105
Essex Station, Boston, MA 02112
866-692-6901 • TTY : 866-346-3642
The Medical Information Bureau is a data bank that collects and shares information with insurance companies. You can request a copy of your file to be sure the information is accurate. Write to Medical Information Bureau or call to obtain a copy of your file. There is no website available.

National Association of Boards of Pharmacy
1600 Feehanville Drive, Mount Prospect, IL 60056
847-391-4406
www.nabp.net
Verifies if an online website is from a licensed pharmacy in good standing with the association. Provides listing of certifies Verified Internet Pharmacy Practice Sites (VIPPS).

National Association for Continence
P.O. Box 1019, Charleston, SC 29402-1019
800-252-3337 • Fax: 843-377-0905
www.nafc.org
Supports the public about the causes, prevention, diagnosis, treatments

and management solutions for incontinence.

National Committee for Quality Assurance
2000 L Street NW #200, Washington, DC 20036
888-275-7585 • Fax: 202-955-3599
www.ncqa.org
Evaluates and accredits Health Maintenance Organizations. Check to see if one is accredited in you area.

National Health Information Center
Brochures on Senior Care and taped explanations of Medicare & Medicaid
1-800-336-4797
http://www.health.gov/nhic

National Kidney Foundation
30 East 33rd Street, New York, NY 10016
800-622-9010
www.kidney.org
Provides health guides on kidney and urinary tract diseases and information on organ donations and transplants for individuals and families affected by these diseases.

National Library of Medicine
8600 Rockville Pike, Bethesda, MD 20894
888-346-3656 • Fax: 301-402-1384 • TTY: 800-735-2258
www.nlm.nih.gov
Collects materials and provides information and research services in all areas of health care. Helps find health information resources, but cannot answer questions about specific medical cases or give medical advice.

National Osteoporosis Foundation
1232 22nd Street NW, Washington, DC 20037-1292
202-223-2226
www.nof.org

Provides educational material which promotes bone health to improve the lives of those affected by osteoporosis and related fractures.

National Stroke Association
9707 E Easter Lane Building B, Englewood, CO 80127
800-787-6537 • Fax: 303-649-1328
www.stroke.org
Provides information about stroke prevention, symptom recognition, treatment options and rehabilitation.

Office of Disability
Department of Health and Human Services
200 Independence Avenue SW Rm 637D
Washington, DC 20201
202-401-5844 • Fax: 202-260-3053
www.hhs.gov/od
Oversees the implementation and coordination of disability programs, policies and special initiatives for persons with disabilities.

Parkinson's Disease Foundation
1359 Broadway Suite 1509, New York, NY 10018
800-457-6676 • Fax: 212-923-4778
www.pdf.org
Provides information, referrals and answers to questions regarding Parkinson's disease.

SeniorClix
Caresource Healthcare Communications, Inc.
2200 Sixth Avenue Suite 833, Seattle, WA 98121
800-448-5213
www.seniorclix.org
An information and e-commerce website focusing on the needs of seniors, family members and caregivers, and the senior services network.

State Health Insurance Counseling and Assistance Programs

www.shiptalk.org
Provides online links to counselors who can answer your questions and help you choose a Medicare plan and/or additional health insurance and help you understand your rights and protections.

Visiting Nurse Associations of America
99 Summer Street Suite 1700, Boston, MA 02110
617-737-3200 • Fax: 617-737-1144
www.vnaa.org
Provides home health care for patients of all ages ranging from child care to hospice care.

HEARING

Better Hearing Institute
515 King Street Suite 420, Alexandria, VA 22314
800-327-9355
www.betterhearing.org
Educates the public about the problem of hearing loss and what can be done about it. Informs persons with impaired hearing and the general public about hearing loss and available help through medicine, surgery and amplification.

Hearing Loss Association of America
7910 Woodmont Avenue Suite 1200, Bethesda, MD 20814
301-657-2248 • Fax: 301-913-9413
www.hearingloss.com
Provides information, education, advocacy and support to people with hearing loss. Publications include information on hearing aids, implants, lip-reading and telephone and television strategies.

Housing

National Reverse Mortgage Lenders Association
1400 16th Street NW #420, Washington, DC 20036
202-939-1760
www.reversemortgage.org
Association of lenders and investors provides information for consumers interested in learning more about using reverse mortgages to convert a portion of a home's equity into cash.

Long-Term Care

American Association of Homes and Services for the Aging
2519 Connecticut Avenue NW, Washington, DC 20008-1520
202-783-2242 • Fax: 202-783-2255
www.aahsa.org
Provides information about aging services and facilities and how to deal with the emotional stresses of care giving, how to plan for long-term case costs and how to get involved in aging services.

National Center for Assisted Living
American Health Care Association
1201 L Street NW, Washington, DC 20005
202-842-4444
www.ahca.org
Provides information on the different types of long term care, how to select the proper level of care and what to look for in a long term care insurance policy.

National Long Term Care Ombudsman Resource Center
1828 L Street NW Suite 801, Washington, DC 20036
202-332-2275 • Fax: 202-332-2949
www.ltcombudsman.org

Educates the consumers about long term care residents' rights and resolves complaints against Long Term Care and Assisted Living facilities.

MEDICARE

Medicare
7500 Security Blvd, Baltimore, MD 21244-1850
800-633-4227 (800-MEDICARE)
www.medicare.gov
Official government information resource on everything about Medicare.

MILITARY AND VETERANS

National Cemetery Administration
Department of Veterans Affairs
810 Vermont Avenue NW, Washington, DC 20420
202-273-5221
www.cem.va.gov
Information about burials, headstones, cemetery grants and presidential memorials. All veterans can receive a burial flag and burial in national cemeteries. Burial at no charge may be possible in area where a national Veterans Cemetery is located.

Tricare
Skyline 5, #810, 5111 Leesburg Pike
Falls Church, VA 22041-3206
Regional Offices:
North: 877-874-2273
South: 800-444-5445
West: 888-874-9378
www.tricare.osd.mil
Provides medical coverage for active duty service personnel and retirees,

their eligible family members and survivors.

Veterans Benefits Administration
Department of Veterans Affairs
810 Vermont Avenue NW, Washington, DC 20420
800-827-1000
www.va.gov
Provides information on veterans' programs including healthcare and has locator for Veterans Affairs facilities worldwide.

Retirement Living

RetirementLiving.com
Compare each state's tax burden, including taxes on retirement income as well as sales, property and estate taxes. Search by state for various housing options including active-adult communities and assisted-living facilities.

BestPlaces.net
Search data on thousands of communities. Use their cost-of-living calculator and compare between communities and cities.

TopRetirements.com
A variety of information is available to help you locate the retirement community right for you, with articles and lists of top-rated retirement communities for you to consider.

FindYourSpot.com
Helps you find a retirement community that is customized to your needs and desires. Take a quiz with dozens of questions regarding your preferred climate, recreation, community size and more and the site will provide you with detailed reports of communities that match your criteria.

GreatPlacesToRetire.com
Lists top cities to retire by category and allows you to search a variety of city reports to help you gather the information you need to make your decision on a city. It will also compare up to three cities side-by-side on issues such as water quality, climate and home values.

ePodunk.com
Browse information on 46,000 communities across the United States. View city tours and read reviews, reports and rankings.

SOCIAL SECURITY

Social Security Administration
Windsor Park Bldg
6401 Security Blvd, Baltimore, MD 21235
800-772-1213 • TTY: 800-325-0778
www.socialsecurity.gov
Official Social Security Administration information resource about applying for Social Security benefits and ordering a Social Security or Medicare card. A Personal Earnings and Benefits Estimate Statement can be requested online. Also provides the address of local Social Security offices, forms to request documents, and a vast amount of additional information on Social Security.

Insurer Rating Companies
The companies listed below rate the financial strength of insurance companies and their ability to meet obligations to policyholders. They offer extensive research, analysis, and ratings information online; some reports may be purchased for offline delivery.

A.M. Best has been providing ratings on most life and health insurance companies for many years. Best's Reports can be found in most libraries.

908.439.2200 ext. 5742
www.ambest.com

Moody's provides ratings for the insurers that request a rating, so these ratings are not available on all insurance companies
212.553.0377
www.moodys.com

Weiss provides safety ratings on almost 2,000 companies
800.289.9222
www.weissratings.com

Standard & Poor provides claims paying ability. They also provide solvency ratings for other insurers. **www2.standardandpoors.com**

Acknowledgments

Writing and teaching have become true passions for me. However, every writer worth his salt realizes that a successful manuscript depends on the insights, support and hard work of others. Below is just a small list of the many people who have helped me, steered me, challenged me, and encouraged me as I attempted this project. I would like to formally thank them for their hard work and direction.

Vicky Guess, my love, my life-partner and wife, and the one who has persevered with me to the completion of this project. Her belief in me has provided me with the determination necessary to see this book to its conclusion.

Melissa Fortenberry, my daughter and operations officer of Senior Financial Services, gave remarkable attention to detail, and provided grammatical and structural thought to the book. Besides that, she has been a rock to keep the company moving forward during the process of writing this book.

Richard Tilford, a great personal friend and partner on the Dollars & Sense radio program, has been a trustworthy sounding board, and reviewed the overall accuracy of content and direction of the manuscript.

Ed Mierzwinski, a consumer advocate in the Washington, D.C.-based federal lobbying office of the National Association of State Public Interest Research Groups (U.S. PIRG) since 1989, and often testifies before both Congress and state legislatures regarding banking, financial services, and identity theft issues. His contribution to the preparation of this manuscript has been invaluable.

Brett Williams, Ph.D., professor at American University and author of Debt for Sale, gave valuable insight, which offered clear direction to my chapters on credit card companies and banks.

Steven N. Weisbart, Ph.D., CLU, Vice President and Chief Economist with Insurance Information Institute, meticulously reviewed the chapter on fixed-indexed annuities. He gave many valuable insights as well as corrections.

Mitzi Werther, Emeritus Program Director at Richland College, provided the opportunity for me to begin educating senior adults on college campuses. Thanks, Mitzi!

Will Gopffarth, Ph.D., has been a God-send. Through the entire writing process, he has provided structural order and organizational insights toward getting my thoughts on paper—a true mentor.

Matt Narramore, author and friend, helped in the thought process of pulling together all the pieces necessary to get the book bound and published.

David Ramsour, international economist, provided valuable

insights to the latest edition.

Retirees who have read the manuscript for ease of reading and importance of content as it relates to their financial lives and needs: Dan Ellis, Gwen Newman, Vernon Winchester and many others. Thank you for your help and support.

Many thanks to those who helped make this book a reality by giving editorial feedback, publishing know-how, and personal encouragement.

Enjoy this?
Check out Bob's other book:

THE KEY TO RESTORING AMERICA

Bob Guess always hated politics. Like most Americans, he lived in a legislative coma.

As a Venture Capitalist, he soon realized that the same building blocks that make a successful business are the same blocks to build a successful country.

The Key to Restoring America teaches the principles that bring unity in diversity, strength in leadership, and hope for our times.

www.RestoringAmerica.com

For more information about protecting
and preserving what you spent a lifetime accumulating,
please visit:

WWW.TEXAS1STFINANCIAL.COM
CALL 972-570-444 OR 866-590-2555